AF378351

EVERTON

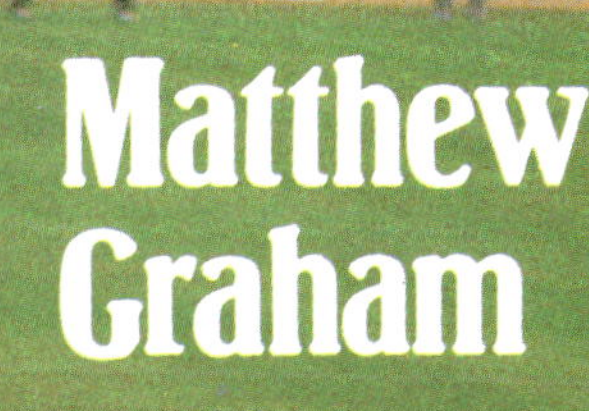

EVERTON

Matthew Graham

HAMLYN

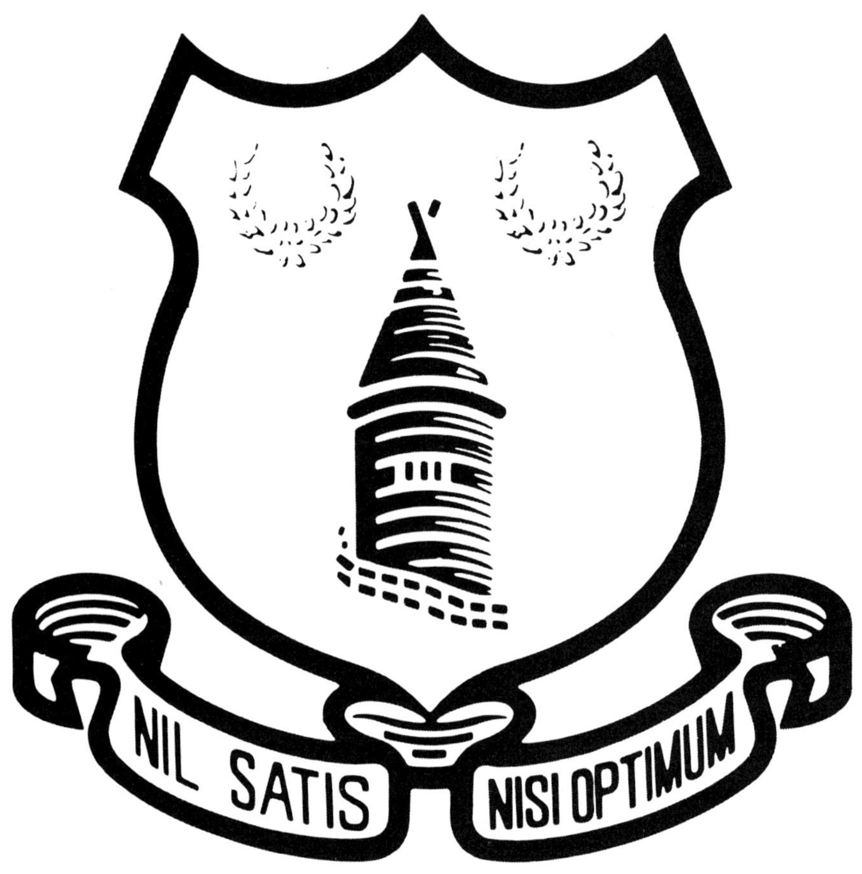

Endpapers *Adrian Heath, and Liverpool's
Bruce Grobbelaar and Alan Kennedy, about to come
together painfully in the 1984 Milk Cup final. It was the
goalkeeper's ball and nobody was injured.*

Title page *Everton, with the FA Cup at Wembley in 1984,
pose for the photographs before their lap of honour.*

Following pages *Andy Gray turns to receive the
congratulations of his team-mates after making sure
Everton will win the Cup, while Terry and Sherwood look
on in disgust from sitting positions.*

Cover photograph *Gary Stevens*

Contents

Published 1986 by
Hamlyn Publishing,
Bridge House, London Road,
Twickenham, Middlesex.

ISBN 0 600 50238 4

Printed in Spain

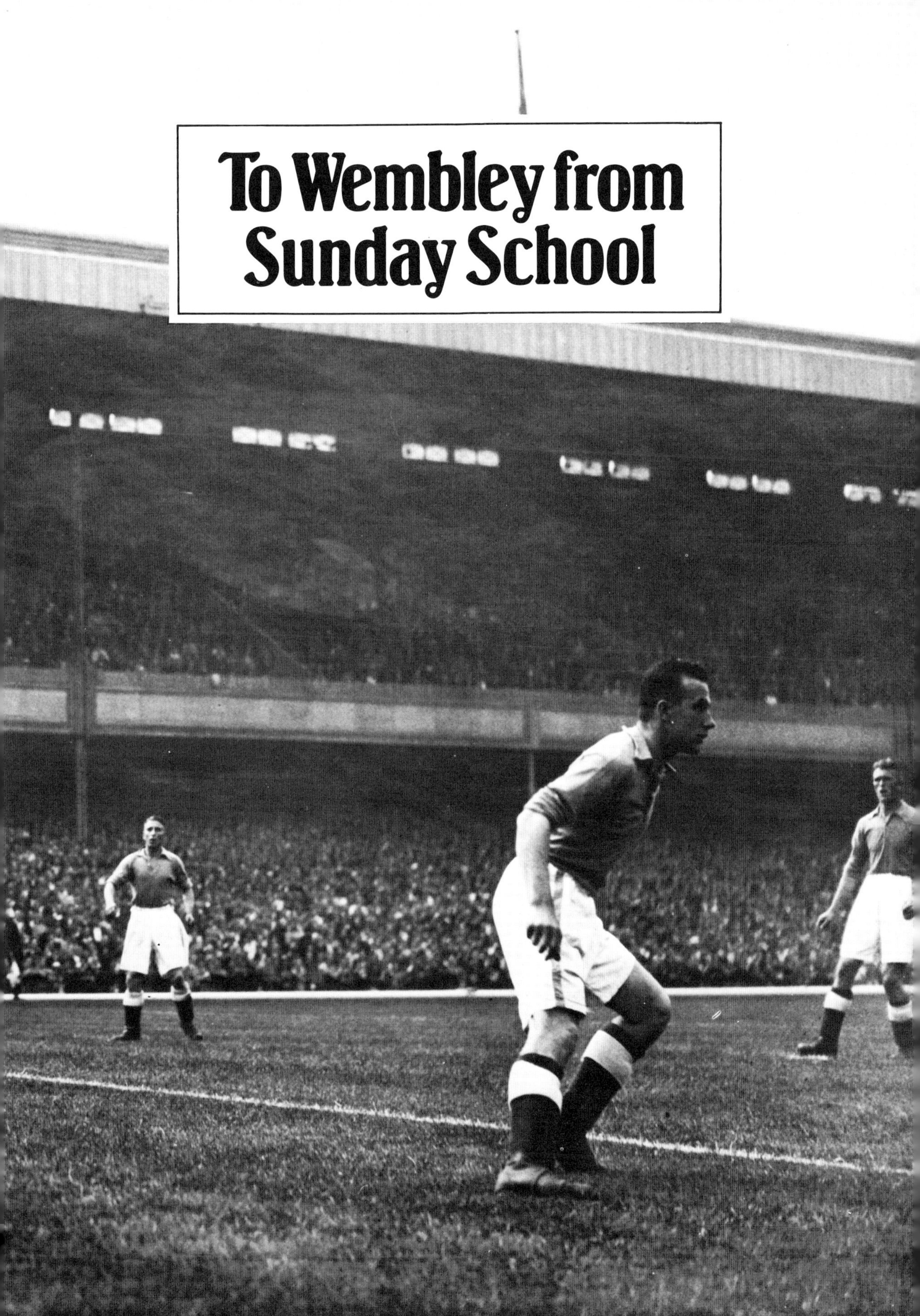

To Wembley from Sunday School

In 1868 a branch of the Methodist Church, called the New Connexion, decided to build a chapel in the well-to-do Everton district of Liverpool. A plot of land was bought on Breckfield Road North, between St Domingo Vale and St Domingo Grove. The first service was held in the new church of St Domingo on 29 May 1870.

Six years later the Rev. B.S. Chambers became minister, and his enthusiasm for sport led to the formation, in 1876, of a cricket club for church and Sunday school members. Two years later the young men of the cricket club formed a football section for the winter.

St Domingo's Football Club played in the south-east corner of Stanley Park. Many junior Sunday sides playing football today will recognize the conditions in which St Domingo's played. There were no changing rooms. Players collected the goalposts from the Park Lodge in Mill Lane and fixed them into sockets in the ground; they also marked out the lines themselves. Naturally anybody could watch. The same circumstances can be seen in parks today all over Great Britain.

The team quickly attracted 'outsiders' who wanted to play – maybe occasionally they were needed to make up the numbers. Again, the same things happen today. It was decided that the team should change its name in order to accommodate non-church members more reasonably. At a meeting at the Queen's Head Hotel, Village Street, in November 1879 the name of the district, Everton, was chosen.

The first match under the new name was played on 20 December 1879, in Stanley Park. The opponents were St Peter's, and Everton won 6–0. That is all that's known of Everton Football Club's first match.

The first known Everton side is that for the second match, also against St Peter's. It is given in the *History of the Everton Football Club*, written by a former director of the club, Thomas Keates, to celebrate the jubilee of the club in 1929. In those days sides were composed mainly of forwards who dribbled the ball forward in a pack, the passing game being an innovation developed by Scottish players that was not universally adopted until a little later. The first known Everton players are thus given as: *Goal:* W. Jones. *Backs:* T. Evans, J. Douglas. *Half-backs:* C. Hiles, S. Chalk (captain). *Forwards:* R.W. Morris, A. White, F. Brettle, A. Wade, Smith, W. Williams.

A. Wade was a director of the club 50 years later. Another link with the club forged early on was that of W.C. Cuff. His father was a pillar of the St Domingo Chapel, and young Will, two years older than Everton, was a choirboy there, and a supporter of the team. Later, he was Secretary, Director and Chairman, serving the club for over 50 years, and leading them to Wembley.

Everton were regarded as the strongest side in Stanley Park and players from other sides (including St Peter's) joined the club. In 1880–81, Everton were admitted to the new Lancashire Football Association.

The new status required a uniform set of shirts. The original colours had been blue and white stripes, but the new players to join had been playing in the shirts they already possessed. The answer was to dye all the shirts black. As this looked unattractive, a wide scarlet sash was added. Everton became known as 'the Black Watch'.

Everton travelled by train to an away match for the first time when they were drawn at Great Lever, from near Bolton, in the Lancashire Cup. Their return journey must have been quite a happy one, as the side had drawn 1–1. The replay at Stanley Park, however, was a revelation: Great Lever won 8–1.

The Football League had not yet been formed at this time. The Football Association was in existence, and the FA Cup competition had begun, as had the international matches with Scotland. These were dominated by the southern sides composed of ex-public school boys, such as the Wanderers and

Old Etonians. Lancashire clubs such as Darwen and the two Blackburn sides, Olympic and Rovers, were about to challenge this superiority.

Everton's third season, 1881–82, opened badly, with a 13–1 defeat by Bolton Wanderers. However, results improved, and the club won 15 of its 22 matches, including a defeat of Cheshire Cup holders Northwich Victoria, and one local paper claimed that, on these results, the 'Moonlight Dribblers' could be regarded as the best team in south-east Lancashire. Perhaps evening practice sessions earned the 'Moonlight Dribblers' nickname.

Everton's 'Black Watch' shirts had soon been discarded. They now played in salmon pink shirts, with blue shorts. These were to be replaced in turn with ruby shirts with blue trim, and dark blue shorts. The famous royal blue came later.

The club had acquired an inspiring captain and coach in Jack McGill, a former Glasgow Rangers player. They were lucky, too, in their secretaries, J.W. Clarke and (from 1882) Tom Evans, a Derbyshire cricketer who was also Everton's vice-captain.

The time soon came to charge admission for the matches, as large crowds watched their games on Stanley Park. The Sandon Hotel, owned by John Houlding, a rich local brewer who was to play an important part in their affairs, had become the headquarters. At a meeting there in March 1882, a Mr Cruitt, of Coney Green, offered the club his field in Priory Road, next to his house. This field was fenced and gated, and Everton arranged to play there in the 1883–84 season, meanwhile playing their last season at Stanley Park.

At Priory Road, a 'dressing-room' shed was built, and a small stand. The first match was a representative one, Liverpool and District v. Walsall and District. Total receipts were 14s (70p), and Priory Road was soon shown to be no quick way to a fortune. Thomas Keates' history set out a financial summary for early years, and the season's receipts were £45. However, wages, etc., were nil.

Results were better than finances in that season, for Everton won their first trophy. It was the second season of the Liverpool Cup: Bootle had beaten Everton in the semi-final the year before. This time Bootle were beaten 5–2 in the semi-final, and Earlestown 1–0 in the final. John Houlding was the new club president, and he received the Cup. Houlding, a prominent citizen who became Lord Mayor of Liverpool, was soon to be known as 'King John of Everton'.

Mr Cruitt, however, was not so keen on the club's success. Despite the low takings at Priory Road, he found the supporters too numerous and noisy and asked the club to find another ground.

They did – a field in Anfield Road, owned by Orrell Brothers, a brewery. It is strange that the club's early fortunes should be so bound to the Sunday school and the breweries!

Everton agreed to keep the walls in repair, pay the taxes, refrain from being a nuisance, and to pay a donation each year to the Stanley Hospital in the name of Mr Orrell. John Houlding assumed the tenancy.

So only one season was played at Priory Road, and the Everton club and supporters transformed the Anfield Road field into a football ground. It was to become one of the most famous in the world.

The first match played there was on 27 September 1884, when Everton beat Earlestown 5–0. A more exciting match was the Liverpool Cup tie with Bootle, with whom Everton enjoyed a rivalry like that of Everton and Liverpool in later years. With no goals after 90 minutes, the teams played an extra half-hour. Bootle scored in 10 minutes, but Everton came back with two goals, the winner coming in the last minute. The scorer, Parry, was carried shoulder-high to the nearby Sandon Hotel, where the players changed before matches. Over £39 was taken at the gate at this one match alone, so the move to Anfield Road was

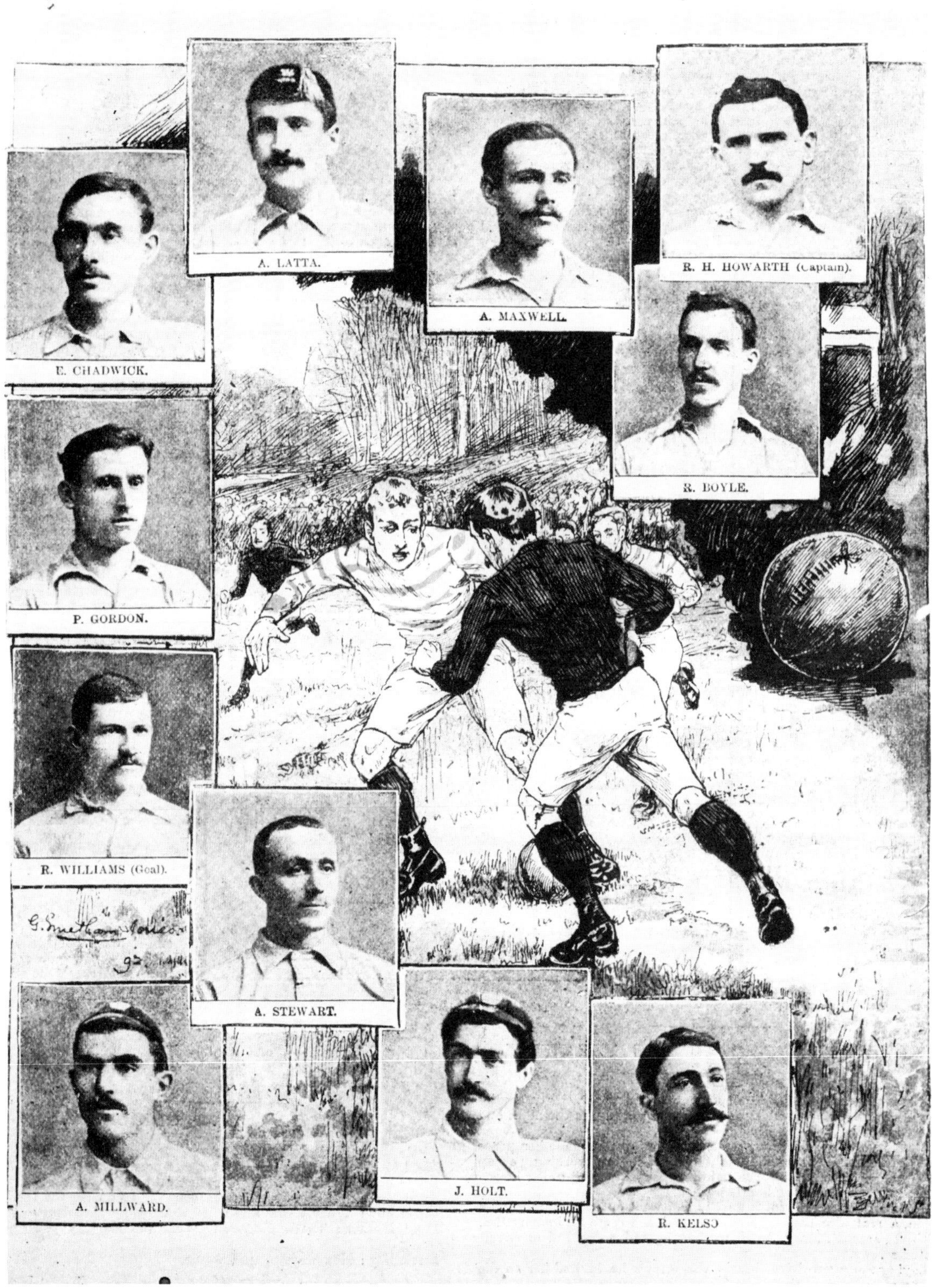

E. CHADWICK.
A. LATTA.
A. MAXWELL.
R. H. HOWARTH (Captain).
R. BOYLE.
P. GORDON.
R. WILLIAMS (Goal).
A. STEWART.
A. MILLWARD.
J. HOLT.
R. KELSO.

already a financial success. The takings for the season were £200.

In the Liverpool Cup final, Everton lost 1–0 to Earlestown, although Everton and the spectators claimed that Everton had scored an equalizer. The referee ruled the ball had passed outside the post, and an angry dispute arose. It was to be a few years yet before nets were invented to preclude such disputes.

In 1885 the Football Association sanctioned professionalism. The question of paid footballers had long been a problem in football. In 1883 Accrington had been disqualified for paying a player in a cup-tie. Preston's president, Major William Sudell, admitted next year that Preston had paid a player too, and Preston were disqualified. Sudell told the FA that all Preston players were professional, but would be amateurs if further trouble arose. The implication was that professionalism, which, in fact, was widespread, would merely go under the counter. The FA first allowed payments for lost wages, at the same time banning Scots from the FA Cup competition, in order to prevent English clubs luring Scottish players south with money. It was no good – after a few months of this, professionalism was legalized.

Everton's first professionals were George Dobson (from Bolton Wanderers) and George Farmer (from Oswestry). A Scot, Alex Dick, followed, Dobson was elected captain, and he and Dick were impressive full-backs: 'their sensational kicking was an entertaining feature of the matches', says Keates. It sounds unsophisticated, and indeed the 'reckless, daring' Dick was given a two-month suspension for foul play.

Everton won the Liverpool Cup again, beating Bootle 2–1, and retained it the following season. This encouraged them to enter the FA Cup in 1886–87, and they were drawn against Glasgow Rangers. Everton lost 1–0 at home in the big event of the season – they had, however, deliberately played ineligible men to make a match of it, so they would not have progressed further anyway.

The following season's FA Cup provided a farce of a tie with the mighty Bolton Wanderers. Everton lost 1–0, then objected to a Bolton player whose registration was found to have occurred three days late. The FA ordered a replay – and after a draw, another, also drawn. Everton won the fourth match, but then Bolton objected to Everton's inducements to 'amateurs'. The complaint was upheld, seven Everton 'amateurs' were declared professional, the Everton ground was shut for one month and Everton were disqualified (although in fact they had already lost 6–0 to Preston in the next round). The Liverpool Association immediately took the Liverpool Cup back, too, collecting it from the Sandon Hotel in a cab. Everton temporarily withdrew from the Liverpool Association in a huff.

Big things began to happen elsewhere, however. The Football League was founded in April 1888, and Everton were one of the 12 sides selected to form it. The others were Accrington, Aston Villa, Blackburn Rovers, Bolton Wanderers, Burnley, Derby County, Notts County, Preston North End, Stoke, West Bromwich Albion and Wolverhampton Wanderers. These were all Lancashire and Midlands clubs, and included the strongest in the country. Each year from 1884 one of these sides had won the FA Cup, and only once since has a non-League club done so: Tottenham Hotspur in 1901.

Everton signed some famous players for the first League season: Johnnie Holt from Bootle, 'Alf Milward from Great Marlow, Edgar Chadwick from Blackburn Rovers and Nick Ross from Preston. The first three won England caps. The first League match was at home, against Accrington, and Everton won 2–1, G. Fleming scoring both goals. The season was disappointing, however, Everton finishing eighth. The following year they improved to second.

In 1890–91 Everton became the second club to win the Championship (Preston won the first two). The players who made this possible were

The side against Aston Villa in the Championship year of 1914–15. Left to right, back: Tom Fleetwood, right-half; Alan Grenyer, reserve; R. Thompson, right-back; Jimmy Galt, centre-half and captain, Scottish international; Tom Fern, goalkeeper; J.S. MacConachie, left-back; Harry Makepeace, left-half, English international. Front row: Sammy Chedgzoy, outside-right, English international; W. Kirsopp, inside-right; Bobby Parker, centre-foward, whose 36 League goals that season made him the First Division's leading scorer; Joe Clennel, inside-left; J. Roberts, outside-left, who played only this one game for Everton. Everton won 5–1 at Villa Park.

principally: J. Angus, D. Jardine, A. Hannah, D. Doyle, D. Kirkwood, J. Holt, W. Campbell, C. Parry, A. Latta, A. Brady, F. Geary, E. Chadwick, A. Milward.

Thomas Keates noted the gate receipts for the previous and following years: £5188 and £5747. Players' wages, etc., were given as £2059 and £4038. In the later year the 12 best-paid players received £3 per week each.

In 1891 a smouldering crisis in the club's affairs flamed up. When the Anfield Road premises were taken, John Houlding, the President, arranged to be the club's representative tenant. However, he had quickly made himself the landlord, and charged the club rent, initially £100 per year.

The Committee wanted a lease on the ground, so that investment in stands and accommodation would benefit the club, not the landlord. Houlding made counter proposals. Thinking he had the upper hand, as the club would not wish to move and forfeit their stands, he raised the rent – to £240 in 1888–89 and £250 in 1889–90.

Members of the Committee decided to fight Houlding and obtained an option on Mere Green field, described as 'a howling desert' in Goodison Road, on the north side of Stanley Park and a short walk from Anfield Road. The club was formed into a limited company, under the name of 'Everton Football Club Limited', with a capital of £500 in £1 shares.

The field cost £8090, and the work needed to make it Goodison Park cost £4000. Seven months after the committee's resolution, on 24 August 1892, Goodison Park was officially opened.

The driving force in Everton's move was George Mahon, an accountant, and the first Chairman of the company. His credentials were immaculate: he was also the organist at St Domingo's Church. A principal helper in raising the money was Dr J.C. Baxter, described by Keates as a Good Samaritan, who was prepared to loan the complete amount, and advanced £1000 without security and free of interest. He, too, joined the board.

The grand opening was inaugurated by a dinner at the old Adelphi Hotel. The Guest of Honour was Lord Kinnaird, who had appeared in a record nine

Cup finals and was to become President of the Football Association. Other soccer dignitaries were present, and all drove in the afternoon to Goodison in open carriages. A crowd of 12,000 watched the parade and a programme of sports events. A band, illuminations and a firework display were among the entertainments.

Meanwhile John Houlding had resolved that he would keep the name Everton at Anfield, and build a new team. But the FA ruled that the name Everton belonged to the new company which contained most of the members of the original club, and Houlding had to call his team by another name – and settled on Liverpool AFC.

In 1893–94, Liverpool were admitted to the new Second Division of the Football League, and won it. The great rivalry between the clubs was therefore soon joined on the pitch, as well as in the back rooms.

Near Goodison Park was Mother Noblett's Toffee Shop, which might have helped Everton get the nickname 'The Toffees' or 'The Toffeemen'. But near the Queen's Head Hotel, where Everton was first named, was also Ye Anciente Everton Toffee House, so there are at least two claimants to the honour.

The first match at Goodison was a friendly against Bolton Wanderers on 2 September 1892. The side, which fought back from two down to win 4–2 was: Jardine, Howarth, Dewar, Boyle, Holt, Robertson, Latta, Maxwell, Geary, Chadwick, Milward.

The first League match was with Nottingham Forest, and was drawn 2–2. The season was successful, Everton finishing third in the table. They also

Sammy Chedgzoy near the end of his career. He once dribbled the ball in direct from a corner-kick and forced a change in the laws.

Warney Cresswell (left) shaking hands with Chelsea skipper Jack Townrow at Stamford Bridge in 1929, before an FA Cup tie which Second-Division Chelsea won 2–0.

reached the Cup final for the first time, losing 1–0 to Wolves. An amusing aside to this was that the teams met in a League match the previous Saturday, and Everton played a reserve side, which won 4–2. Gate receipts for the club in the first Goodison season were £8815, and players' wages, etc., were £3539, so much of Goodison's initial outlay was returning quickly.

Season 1895–96 was a traumatic one for Everton. McMahon and four other directors resigned over administration problems. There was also a turnstile swindle. Suspicions had been voiced that the estimated crowds and the turnstile returns did not tally. For the Sunderland match on 12 December 1895 a director and the groundsman noted the turnstile starting numbers half-an-hour before the gates opened, as was customary. However, on this day the numbers were checked again by two directors 20 minutes later, and it was discovered that several turnstiles had been moved back 200 units. The 'Everton Turnstiles Fraud' was a sensation of the day, and about 15 conspirators, including the groundsman, appeared in court. Will Cuff was one of the new directors who joined the board after the resignations.

Later that month there was a riot after the referee had allowed a game to proceed on a pitch made into a swamp by three days of rain. After 30 minutes the match was abandoned. Some of the crowd demanded their money back, and were reinforced, according to Keates, by an army of street loafers taking advantage of the situation. Although they were offered free tickets for the replay, a riot ensued, windows and woodwork were smashed, and there was a move to fire the stands before contingents of police arrived to drive the mob away with batons.

In 1897 Everton reached the Cup final again, and lost 3–2 to Aston Villa, in what was described as the best Cup final played until then. That season Villa became the second club after Preston to achieve the League and Cup 'double'.

After 10 years of the Football League, Everton could claim to be the second most successful side in the country behind Villa. Curiously, Keates claimed that they had scored 324 goals, second only to Villa's 326. This mistake has been perpetuated in two of the best modern histories. In fact Everton won 324 *points*, second to Villa's 339.

Among new personnel at Goodison around the turn of the century were 'Sandy' Young, a dashing centre-forward; and Dr Leigh Roose, known as 'Dickie', an eccentric goalkeeper, who made as big an impression as Bruce Grobbelaar does at Anfield today. Other prominent newcomers were Jack Sharp, Walter Abbott and Jimmy Settle.

The team was strangely inconsistent, finishing League runners-up in 1902 and 1905, and at last winning the FA Cup, in 1906, in a match described in Chapter 5. H.P. Hardman, their brilliant amateur left-winger that day, later became a director of the club. In between these seasons Everton had some poor League placings.

A Cup-final defeat by Sheffield Wednesday in 1907 was followed by another poor season, then another League runners-up berth.

In the last season before the First World War, Everton finally won their second League Championship. Two new players had much to do with it: Bobby Parker, a centre-forward from Rangers, whose 36 goals headed the League scoring list, and Tom Fern, a goalkeeper from Lincoln City. Other stalwarts were captain Jimmy Galt, another recent signing from Rangers, at centre-half, Sam Chedgzoy, the brilliant right-winger, and Harry Makepeace at wing-half.

Jimmy Dunn, the Scottish international inside-forward who delighted the fans with clever play in the early 1930s.

Above *Neil McBain (centre), a wing-half of the 1920s. In March 1947 he became the oldest Football League player, turning out for New Brighton in goal aged 52 years 4 months.*

Opposite below *Everton in 1926–27: 20th in the League, but Champions next year. Left to right, back: F. Kennedy, inside-left; J. O'Donnell, left-back; W. Brown, right-half; Bert Hardy (goalkeeper); Hunter Hart, captain and centre-half; John McDonald, right-back; Harry Cooke, trainer. Front: T. Millington, outside-right; Bobby Irvine, inside-right and Irish international; Dixie Dean, centre-forward and English international; A.A. Dominy, inside-left; Alec Troup, Scottish international outside-left; Albert Virr, left-half. Only Dean, Hart, O'Donnell, Troup and Virr were regulars in the Championship side of 1927–28.*

The war, of course, upset many playing careers and there were many new faces in the Everton side when League football resumed in 1919–20. There were now 22 First-Division sides – the following season there was a new Third Division, and the season after that two Third Divisions, split into North and South. Professional football was becoming even more competitive. Everton were only one position above relegation in 1921–22 and after moving up and down the table were 20th again in 1926–27. But on 16 March 1925 Everton had signed the most famous player in their history.

'Give it to Dixie' was a cry becoming famous at Tranmere Rovers in 1924–25, where an 18-year-old Billy 'Dixie' Dean scored an average of a goal a game for 27 matches before Everton paid £3000 for him.

Dean earned a regular place soon after the start of the following season, netting 32 goals in 38 League matches. This was the first season of the new off-side rule, by which an attacker, to be on-side, needed to have only two defenders between himself and the opposing goal when the ball was played. Previously the number had been three. Consequently, before defences perfected a plan to stop attackers (the stopper centre-half was soon invented) there was an upsurge in goalscoring. The following season, 1926–27, George Camsell, of Second-Division Middlesbrough, netted a record 59 goals in League football, including 29 in 12 matches.

After their depressing season in 1926–27, the next was to be one of the greatest in Everton's history. It was also the greatest in Dean's career, despite his being nearly killed in a motorcycle accident in the preceding summer.

Dixie started by scoring in the first nine matches as follows: 1, 1, 1, 2, 1, 2, 2, 2, 5. This last was in a 5–2 defeat of Manchester United at Goodison.

On 29 October Everton led the Championship, and stayed top until 10 March, when they had hit a slide of nine games without a win. However, April saw them winning again, and they fought back to the leadership.

With Dean scoring again, it became a possibility that he could beat Camsell's new record. With seven games left, he needed 15 goals. With three games left, he still wanted nine. He scored twice in a 3–2 defeat of Aston Villa, and then gave himself a real chance with four in a 5–3 win at Burnley. With Arsenal to visit Goodison in the last match, he had 57 goals and needed a hat-trick; Everton were already sure of the Championship.

Thomas Keates described the hope that brought 'upwards of 60,000' to Goodison that day, 'simmering with excitement'. After two minutes Arsenal were ahead. A minute later Dixie's famous head had equalized. After five more minutes, Dean was brought down, and scored from the spot – the record was now tied. Ten minutes from half-time Arsenal equalized.

The excitement continued to simmer until eight minutes from the end. Alec Troup took a corner for Everton and Dixie's 'magical head' tipped it in. Keates says: '...we have never heard such a prolonged roar of thundering, congratulatory applause before as that which ascended to heaven when 'Dixie' broke the record'. Another report says the cheering lasted to the end of the game.

There was also what Keates calls a 'comic episode'. A 'low-looking comedy chap' evaded the police and shook Dixie's hand. A 'second comedian' then appeared and kissed him. 'The patience of the referee was exhausted: he seized the second comedian by the scruff of the neck and bundled him off the ground. While the unrehearsed comedy was being enacted, screams of

Above *Albert Geldard, the youngest Football League player (for Bradford PA) at 15 years 156 days, later spent six seasons at Everton and won four England caps.*

Billy Cook, the Irish·international full-back who spent seven seasons at Everton, his last being the Championship year of 1938–39.

Preceding pages *The 1938–39 Champions, who reigned for eight years, because of the war. Left to right, back: Tommy Lawton, Dixie Dean's centre-forward replacement and an England international; Tommy G. Jones, centre-half and Welsh international; Ted Sagar, winnin; his second Championship medal; trainer Harry Cooke, with his third Championship side; Joe Mercer, England international, playing right-half this season; Norman Greenhalgh, ever-present left-back. Front: Billy Cook, right-back; Torry Gillick, Scottish international outside-right; Stan Bentham, deep-lying roving inside-right; Jock Thomson, left-half; Alex Stevenson, Irish international; Wally Boyes, a tiny outside-left.*

Warney Cresswell, the full- back Everton bought from Sunderland in 1927 and who helped them win the Championship in 1927–28.

laughter mingled with the storm of applause'.

It must have been a great day, not spoiled by Arsenal equalizing again in the last minute.

The Championship side was: Arthur Davies, the goalkeeper; the classy Warney Cresswell and Jack O'Donnell at full-back; Jack Kelly, from Ayr, Hunter Hart and local-boy Albert Virr at half-back; Ted Critchley, engaged for the accuracy of his centres, on the right-wing; Dick Forshaw, bought from Liverpool, and Tony Weldon from Airdrie, at inside-forward; the great Dixie Dean at centre-forward; and little Alec Troup, also renowned for his accuracy in finding Dean's head, on the left-wing.

Alas, this great success did not last. Unaccountably, the team dropped to 18th next season, and in 1929–30 they finished bottom, and were relegated for the first time. The shame lasted only a season, for Everton won the Second Division at the first time of asking, and came straight back – to such effect that they won the First Division straight away. They were high scorers: Leicester City were beaten 9–2, Sheffield Wednesday 9–3, Newcastle 8–1, Chelsea 7–2, and West Ham 6–1, while several sides conceded five.

Of the Championship side of four years earlier, Cresswell, Critchley and Dean remained, Dixie scoring 45 goals. Other principal players were Jimmy Dunn, one of the famous Scottish 'Wembley Wizards'; Ted Sagar, the record one-club man, playing his first full season in goal (his career lasted over 24 years); Charlie Gee, a strong 'stopper' centre-half; Ben Williams, right-back and captain; Archie Clark and Jock Thomson from Dundee at wing-half; Tosh Johnson from Manchester City, who became Dean's goalscoring lieutenant; and Jimmy Stein, another Scot, on the left-wing.

Everton's improvement was maintained in 1932–33, when they won the FA Cup for the second time. The victory over Manchester City is described in Chapter 5. New regulars were Billy Cook at full-back, Cliff Britton, a cultured right-half, Tommy White at centre-half, and Albert Geldard on the right-wing. He signed for Everton from Bradford Park Avenue, where he had become the youngest-ever League player at 15 years 156 days in 1929. Strangely, Neil McBain, an Everton full-back of the 1920s, became the oldest League player in 1947, when as manager of New Brighton he was forced to play in goal when 52 years 4 months old.

For the next five years Everton dithered and did little, except to acquire some players who became famous Evertonians, principally Joe Mercer, who became a regular at left-half in 1935–36, and Tommy Lawton, often bracketed with Dean at the top of the list of great centre-forwards. He was signed for the colossal sum for a 17-year-old of £6500 in March 1937. Everton also signed Bobby Bell, whose nine goals for Tranmere against Oldham on Boxing Day 1935 was a League record until Joe Payne scored 10 for Luton at Easter.

Everton were rebuilding as Dean and Cresswell approached the end of their careers. In 1938–39 they won the Championship again, rising from 14th place the previous season. They were never out of the first two, and won by four points from Wolves, their only serious challengers.

Sagar was in goal; Cook still at right-back; Norman Greenhalgh, once singled out by Stanley Matthews as his hardest opponent, at left-back; Joe Mercer was now playing right-half; Tommy G. Jones, the Welsh international, centre-half; John Thomson won his place back at left-half in his last season; Torry Gillick, a fast Scottish right-winger, made trickery and entertainment his forte, as players like Shackleton, Marsh and Bowles have since; Stan Bentham was at inside-forward and later joined the staff; Tommy Lawton was at centre-forward; Alex Stevenson, the tiny Irish international, inside-left; and Wally Boyes, one of the smallest of all wingers at 5ft 3in. (1.60m) and a box of tricks, was outside-left. He made two appearances for England in this season, but could not re-establish himself after the war.

Everton were one of the last clubs to appoint a manager when Theo Kelly took the job at the end of this season. He had been secretary for some years. Unfortunately his prime task became to organize wartime matches, as the Second World War ended all thoughts of serious football. Everton remained Champions for eight years, just as they had been Champions for six years from 1915.

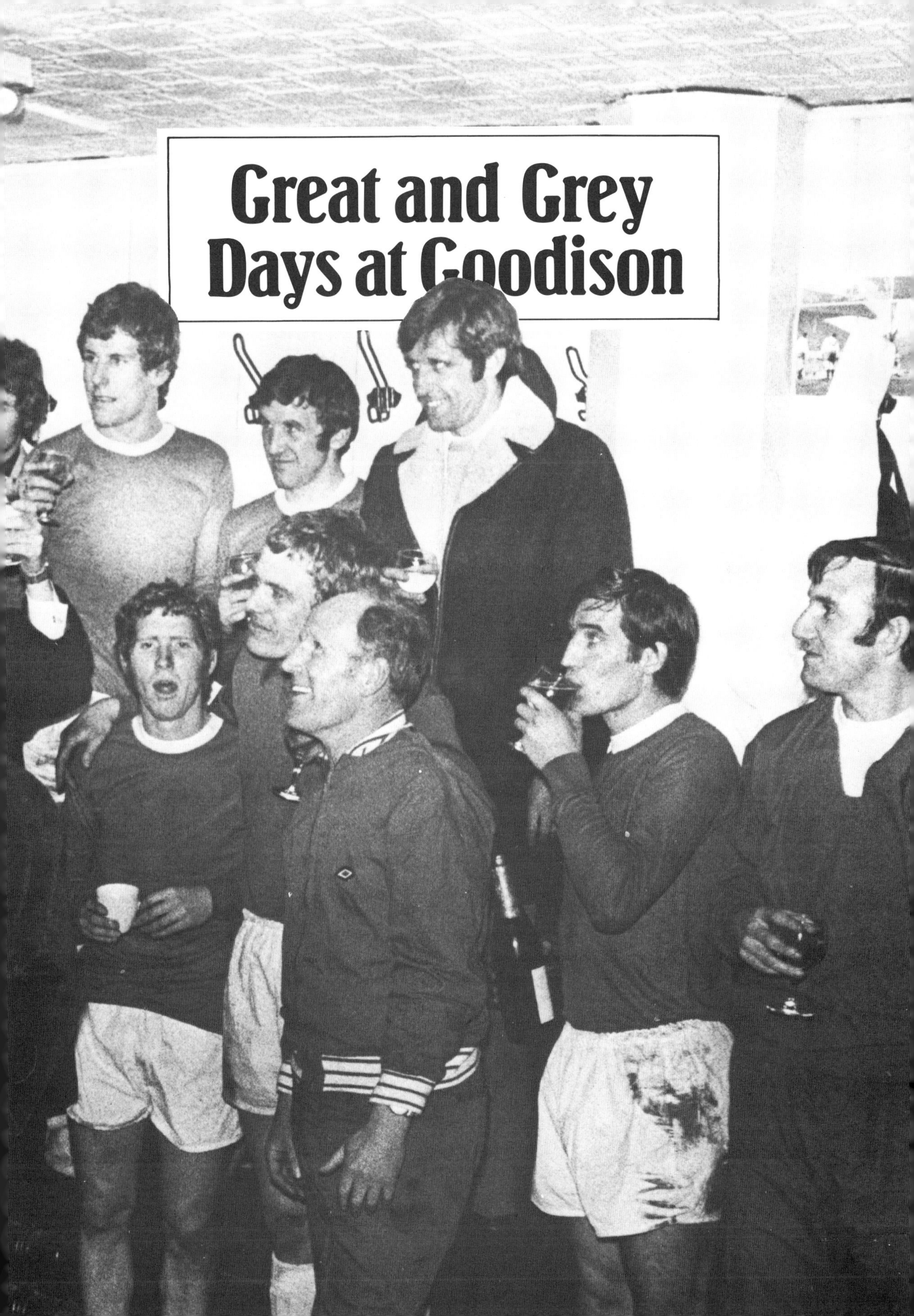

Great and Grey
Days at Goodison

During the Second World War, football was regionalized and players, most of whom were in the services, turned out as 'guests' for teams near their stations. The most famous example is of Everton's Britton and Mercer joining up with Wolves' Stan Cullis and making Aldershot one of the strongest of wartime teams with the England half-back line on call. Many players, including these and Tommy Lawton, distinguished themselves in unofficial wartime internationals, which are not included in the records. When Lawton was unavailable for Everton, his deputy for the Blues was often a youngster from Darlington, Harry Catterick, who later became a successful Everton manager.

Attendances boomed after the war, when there was a season of transition in 1945–46, involving full regional league programmes. The FA Cup resumed, and there was disaster at Burnden Park, with 33 killed and 500 injured when crowds pressed through the gates to see Bolton play Stoke City.

Everton's first team on the resumption of the Championship in 1946–47 was: Burnett, Jackson, Greenhalgh, Mercer, T.G. Jones, Watson, McIlhatton, Wainwright, Catterick, Fielding, Boyes. So only four regulars from the Championship side began the new campaign as Brentford won 2–0 at Goodison. Sagar returned later, but a restless Tommy Lawton had already departed for good – transferred to Chelsea in November 1945.

It was said that manager Theo Kelly was not popular with the players – Mercer became very depressed and was contemplating retirement when Arsenal signed him in December 1946. He enjoyed great success with the London club.

Kelly sought Albert Stubbins from Newcastle to fill the Dean/Lawton role, but Liverpool bought him instead and won the Championship. Kelly settled for Jock Dodds, Scotland's wartime centre-forward, from Blackpool. His best signing was the double one of Peter Farrell, who became captain, and Tommy Eglington, from Shamrock Rovers – two lively, happy players who gave Everton character in the first post-war years.

Goodison fans needed something to enliven the gloom. Just as after the First World War, the Champions' form went from bad to worse. In that first season Everton finished 10th, then dropped to 14th. Theo Kelly returned to the secretaryship and Cliff Britton, who had been managing Burnley, returned as manager. In the same month, September 1948, Everton recorded their highest attendance: 78,299 for the visit of Liverpool. The match was drawn 1–1.

In seasons 1948–49 and 1949–50, Everton were 18th in the League. In the latter season they enjoyed a Cup run to the semi-final. Their opponents at Maine Road were Liverpool, who beat Everton 2–0 and went to Wembley.

In 1949 Will Cuff, the choirboy at St Domingo's over 60 years earlier, and who became Chairman, died. He did not see Everton's relegation into the Second Division for the second time. On the last day of the 1950–51 season, Everton were 20th, two points above Sheffield Wednesday and Chelsea. They visited Wednesday needing a point to stay up. Wednesday won 6–0, Chelsea won 4–0, and because all of them had 32 points, Chelsea stayed up on goal average by 0.04 of a goal.

Meanwhile, Dave Hickson had signed from Ellesmere Port and was to become very popular in the Second Division as a blond, aggressive centre-forward, particularly good in the air. This time, Everton failed to come straight back, and indeed in 1952–53 sank to 16th place, the lowest in their history.

A Cup run, however, took them to the semi-final, where Bolton Wanderers were the opponents at Maine Road. In an extraordinary match, Bolton, inspired by Nat Lofthouse, led 4–0 at half-time, but Everton came back to lose only by 4–3. Bolton lost the final 4–3 to Blackpool, in 'Stanley Matthews' Match'.

The following season Everton won their last match against Oldham 4–0 to

secure second place in the table and promotion. The team at this time was: O'Neill, Donovan, Lindsay, Farrell, T.E. Jones, Lello, Wainwright, Fielding, Hickson, Parker, Eglington. Liverpool took Everton's place in the Second Division.

During the remainder of the 1950s, Everton occupied a lowly place in the top flight. In 1956 Cliff Britton, after a broad hint from the board, resigned. Ian Buchan was appointed as team coach, without the full powers of a manager, and although he might have succeeded as a manager, he could achieve little in his two years before Johnny Carey, the former Manchester United player, was appointed manager. Bobby Collins had recently been bought from Celtic, and there was the nucleus of a promising side at Goodison.

The result at White Hart Lane on 11 October 1958 might not have indicated so, however. Everton suffered their biggest defeat, 10–4, at the hands of Spurs. More significantly, John Moores, the football pools millionaire, became a benefactor of the club, eventually becoming Chairman.

Carey was able to bring to Goodison Alex Young, a clever forward from Hearts, Roy Vernon, Blackburn's young Welsh international striker, and Jimmy Gabriel, a powerful wing-half from Dundee. In 1960–61 the Blues rose to fifth in the Championship.

Progress was not fast enough, however, for in 1961 Carey was offered a golden handshake by John Moores. The offer was made in the back of a taxi which they took from the Football League AGM in London. For the next few years the joke aimed at Everton managers when the team was having a lean time was 'send for a taxi'.

The Everton first-team squad for 1954–55, the first season back in the First Division. Left to right, back: Cliff Britton, manager; Jackie Grant, Central League side captain; Eric Moore, right-back; Tommy E. Jones, long-serving centre-half; Jimmy O'Neill, a Republic of Ireland international goalkeeper; Don Donovan, left-back and another Republic of Ireland international; Cyril Lello, left-half; C. Leyfield, trainer. Front: Tony McNamara, outside-right; Wally Fielding, inside-right; Eddie Wainwright, who played inside-right and outside-right; Peter Farrell, the right-half and captain who played for both Irish teams; Tommy Eglington, outside-left, who also played for the Republic and Northern Ireland; Dave Hickson, centre-forward; John Willie Parker, inside-left.

John Moores, the Littlewoods football pools millionaire, in his seat at Goodison. He was a great influence in the late 1960s as backer and director, and helped build the Championship-winning side of 1969–70.

Harry Catterick, the old Everton forward who was manager of Sheffield Wednesday, took over at Goodison, with instructions from Moores to get to the top with good football. The request might have prompted a cynical laugh, but that is just what Catterick achieved.

In 1961–62 Everton finished fourth in the table, while Liverpool, under their new manager, Bill Shankly, were moving up from the Second Division.

In 1962–63, in a season of bad weather, Everton won the Championship for the sixth time. Never out of the first three, they remained unbeaten at home.

The Championship winners were: Gordon West, a recent buy from Blackpool; Alex Parker, a classic full-back from Falkirk in his fifth season with Everton; Mick Meagan, a Republic of Ireland international, as his partner, Jimmy Gabriel at right-half; Brian Labone at centre-half; Brian Harris initially, then Tony Kay, at left-half; Billy Bingham, the Irish international, then Alex Scott, the Scottish international bought from Rangers in mid-season, at outside-right; Dennis Stevens, an ever-present, at inside-right; Alex Young, the other ever-present, at centre-forward; Roy Vernon, the Welsh international who captained the side, at inside-left; and Johnny Morrissey at outside-left.

If Scott was a good buy, Kay was disastrous. Catterick had made him captain in his previous job at Wednesday, and paid £60,000 to bring him to Goodison. After winning his Championship medal, he won his first and only cap for England as a tough, constructive midfield player. In January 1965, however, Kay, with nine other players and former players, was convicted of fixing matches while at Wednesday, and banned for life. Catterick never accepted the injustice of the penalty to Everton for a crime committed at Sheffield Wednesday.

Catterick left the Championship celebrations to drive to Scotland and sign Sandy Brown, a utility player from Partick Thistle. An earlier visit to Scotland had been less fruitful. In Everton's first European campaign, in the Inter-Cities Fairs Cup (later the UEFA Cup), Dunfermline had beaten them 2–0 to overcome a 1–0 advantage Everton had achieved at Goodison.

In 1963–64 Everton were in the European Cup itself, but got no change from Inter Milan, the eventual winners, in the first round. In a typical Italian display Inter drew 0–0 at Goodison and won 1–0 in Milan. Colin Harvey made his debut in the second leg. Everton finished third in the League – Liverpool were Champions.

Two important signings were made for the following season: Fred Pickering, a converted full-back, was bought from Blackburn Rovers to lead the attack – he was soon to win an England cap – and Ray Wilson, the long-time England left-back, was signed from Huddersfield.

The season included a bitter match with Don Revie's Leeds United, for whom the combative Bobby Collins now played. Sandy Brown was sent off in the opening minutes of a savage encounter, and Derek Temple was carried off after a tackle by Willie Bell. Leeds' win-at-all costs reputation was still in its infancy, but their gamesmanship seems to have provoked a match so violent that the referee was forced to take the players off the field for a cooling-down period.

Everton finished fourth this season, and the following season had dropped to 11th, but they reached the Cup final for the first time in 33 years. Harry Catterick found himself the victim of an assault by fans when he omitted Alex Young, the 'Golden Vision' and idol of the crowd, to introduce the young Joe Royle at Blackpool in November. Everton lost 2–0, and an element of the visiting supporters was far from pleased.

In the Cup run it took three matches to dispose of Manchester City. Manchester United were to be faced in the semi-final but before this Everton were due to visit Leeds United. Even more outrageously than before the 1893 final, Everton fielded a complete reserve side. This time they lost 4–1, and were fined £2000 by the League.

Actually, one of these reserves did play at Wembley. Mike Trebilcock, who scored Everton's goal, retained his place in the semi-final in preference to Pickering, who had scored in every round till then, and although Pickering got back into the League side, Trebilcock surprisingly kept him out of the final. Everton were the first side for 63 years to reach the final without conceding a goal; Wednesday only the second this century to get there without a home draw. Trebilcock's part in this remarkable final is described in Chapter 5. Liverpool's League triumph provided a Merseyside double to equal that of 60 years earlier.

England's World Cup win followed in the summer. The strongest group was based at Goodison, where regulars saw the brilliant matches between Portugal, Brazil and Hungary, whose centre-forward, Florian Albert, almost ousted Alex Young in their affections.

The man Harry Catterick had his eye on, however, was Alan Ball, and he beat Don Revie to it in obtaining his transfer from Blackpool for a record £110,000.

Everton were sixth in the table the next season, and reached the sixth round of the Cup, beating Liverpool 1–0 at Goodison on the way. Next year they moved up to fifth, and reached Wembley again, only to lose disappointingly 1–0 to West Bromwich Albion.

By now Howard Kendall had arrived from Preston at right-half, and John Hurst, Jimmy Husband and Joe Royle had found regular places in the side. The Wembley team was: West, Wright, Wilson, Kendall, Labone, Harvey, Husband, Ball, Royle, Hurst, Morrissey.

Throughout their history Everton have been renowned for their clever,

Jimmy Husband, a skilful Geordie at his best in the late 1960s, beating a tackle by Leeds' Jack Charlton.

controlled play. Science has always been preferred to brawn by club and fans alike. Now they began to play as sweetly as at any time in their history, largely due to the understanding which developed between their midfield triangle of Kendall, Harvey and Ball. To which, said Catterick, should be added 'safety-valve' winger Morrissey, always available to take the ball and hold it when all attacking options were temporarily closed down.

The Cup-final side, with Sandy Brown taking the place of Ray Wilson, whose distinguished career ended with a training injury to his leg, finished third in the 1968–69 Championship, and reached the FA Cup semi-final, losing 1–0 to Joe Mercer's Manchester City, who went on to take the Cup.

Season 1969–70 was the peak for this great side. They led the League for most of the season, playing hard but attractive football, and when there was a sticky patch in January, and Leeds got to the top, they produced a match-winning reserve in small fair-haired Alan Whittle, who deputized for Husband and Ball before making the No. 7 shirt his own. He played 15 games, scored 11 goals

One Spur down, and Mike England and Pat Jennings at panic stations as Joe Royle, Everton's England international centre-forward, prepares to strike.

and ensured that Everton galloped away from the opposition to win by nine points from Leeds, who also lost the Cup final to Chelsea.

Everton fans thought that this side might go on to great things, but something went drastically wrong. Next season they slid down the table to 14th as Arsenal became the team of the moment by achieving the 'double'. They might have faced Arsenal at Wembley but lost the Cup semi-final to Liverpool. Meanwhile their second attack on the European Cup failed when, after beating Borussia Moenchengladbach on penalties in the second round, they lost to Panathinaikos, of Greece, on away goals in the third.

Goodison Park received its biggest improvement in 1971. The current three-decker main stand was built at a cost of £1 million. The Bullens Road stand was re-roofed, and the old floodlights were replaced by the powerful banks of lights on the roofs. Always one of the best grounds in the country, Goodison Park is now one of the best in Europe.

On the pitch, Henry Newton, a classy full-back from Nottingham Forest,

had been signed, and Roger Kenyon had finally taken over from Brian Labone at centre-half, but the team's form did not improve. In December 1971, after a defeat by Derby County had dropped the Blues to 18th place, Catterick sold Alan Ball to Arsenal for another record, £220,000. Soon after, driving back from watching a match at Sheffield, Catterick had a heart attack. Despite being in intensive care for a while, he returned to work in 10 weeks.

The side finished 15th. Other players were signed, including striker Joe Harper from Aberdeen for £180,000, bought to replace Royle, who was injured in October 1972 and did not play again that season. Mike Bernard had earlier come from Stoke City and John Connolly from St Johnstone. But the side sank further to 17th in 1972–73. Alan Whittle, once thought to be a new Denis Law, proved inconsistent and went to Crystal Palace for £100,000. In April 1973 Catterick, who had returned from illness too quickly, was given an executive role, and the following month another ex-player, Billy Bingham, took over as manager.

There was a further change-round of players, as Newton and Harper left. Dave Clements, the Northern Ireland international, was Bingham's first signing, for £60,000 from Sheffield Wednesday. Late in the season Bob Latchford, a prolific scorer at centre-forward, was bought from Birmingham City for £350,000. Kendall departed in part-exchange.

Results improved and Everton moved up to seventh, and next season, when

Martin Dobson, a polished wing-half, was bought from Burnley for £300,000, they improved further to fourth. Mick Lyons, too, was by now an enthusiastic regular prepared to run and tackle in any position for the club. Colin Harvey and Joe Royle had departed.

Bingham signed Andy King from Luton Town at the end of the 1975–76 season, and in December 1976 added the clever attacker Duncan McKenzie and the midfield player Bruce Rioch to the squad. However, the following month, as Everton languished in 13th place, Bingham was sacked and Gordon Lee took over. Lee was the tough, forceful 'players' man' type of manager who had succeeded as manager at Newcastle United. Lee soon signed the fierce-tackling full-back Mike Pejic from Stoke City for £150,000.

Everton improved to ninth in the table in 1976–77 and had two long and exciting Cup runs, both of which ended in disappointments. In the League Cup they reached the final and after two draws with Aston Villa faced them in a second replay at Old Trafford.

It was an exciting game. After leading, falling behind, and equalizing, Everton lost to a goal two minutes from the end of extra-time.

The FA Cup semi-final was even more disappointing. Liverpool were the opponents at Maine Road. The Everton side at the time was: David Lawson, who was Britain's most expensive goalkeeper when bought from Huddersfield in 1972; Terry Darracott, a local player who was in and out of the side for 11 years; Mike Pejic; Mick Lyons; Ken McNaught, a tall blond centre-half who soon went to Aston Villa for £200,000; Bruce Rioch; Mick Buckley, another local player; Martin Dobson; Jim Pearson, a £100,000 Bingham buy from St Johnstone; Duncan McKenzie; and Ronnie Goodlass, who was born near Goodison Park and was having his best season.

A young David Johnson playing against Derby County. He had three seasons at Goodison in the early 1970s, left for Ipswich, Liverpool and an international career at centre-forward, and returned to Goodison 10 years later.

The match still rankles with Everton fans. McKenzie and Rioch in turn equalized goals from McDermott and Case and then Bryan Hamilton, substituting for Dobson, 'scored' a winner, only for Clive Thomas, a referee who seemed to attract controversy, to declare him off-side. Much discussion and TV slow-motion analysis failed to convince Evertonians that they had not beaten Liverpool. They lost the replay (there was another disputed decision). This was the season Liverpool just missed the 'treble', winning the Championship and European Cup.

John Moores retired from the board in 1977. He and Catterick had put Everton on a pinnacle, from which sadly they slipped almost before they knew they were there.

Manager Lee worked his hardest to take Everton back, but after two seasons in which they finished third and fourth, in 1979–80 they slumped to 19th.

Rioch, McKenzie and King departed rapidly. Expensive buys were striker Mickey Walsh from Blackpool and polished England defender Colin Todd from Derby, both for £300,000. Geoff Nulty, a versatile defender and cheap at £40,000 from Newcastle, was carried off in a 1980 match with Liverpool and did not play again.

The brightest spot in the late 1970s was a 1–0 victory at Goodison in October 1978 over Liverpool, who were dominating English and European football. Before this, Everton had not beaten their local rivals in any competition for seven years.

Lee won nothing with Everton. As football moved into the 1980s he bought established players Brian Kidd and Peter Eastoe, then tried Gary Stanley, Asa Hartford, John Gidman and Gary Megson, all good players, but at the end of the 1980–81 season, with Everton a disappointing 15th, he was sacked.

Howard Kendall, Everton's old favourite, had meanwhile proved his management skills at Blackburn Rovers, bringing them from the Third

Division to near the top of the Second Division. In May 1981 he returned to Goodison as manager.

Kendall was not an immediate Messiah, although the club rose to eighth place in his first season. His first group of signings proved hasty and ill-considered: Alan Biley, Mick Ferguson, Alan Ainscow and Mike T. Walsh from Bolton. Neville Southall, Kevin Richardson and £700,000 Adrian Heath, although the first of these was soon loaned to Port Vale, were better investments.

Kendall found Graeme Sharp and Kevin Ratcliffe already on the books. Kevin Sheedy broke an unwritten agreement that players did not move from one Liverpool club to the other when joining Everton in June 1982 for £100,000. Two months later, another ex-Liverpool player, David Johnson, was brought back to Everton for a second spell to bring some experience to the attack. Kendall also brought back Andy King for a second term at Goodison.

Local boy Gary Stevens eased his way into the side gradually after his debut in October 1981. Graeme Sharp established his place in 1981–82, and Kevin Ratcliffe, after playing left-back, found his true central defensive role in 1982–83. In June 1982, Derek Mountfield was bought from Tranmere Rovers for £30,000 and in December, Kendall made another of his best purchases when paying Bolton £60,000 for Peter Reid. John Bailey and Mark Higgins had become regulars in the side, and Billy Wright and Steve McMahon were still playing well from Gordon Lee's team.

Yet though Everton fought to the sixth round of the FA Cup in 1982–83 before losing 1–0 at Old Trafford, and had established themselves in the top eight in the Division, they still had won nothing. Season 1983–84 would be make-or-break for Howard Kendall.

In the summer, Trevor Steven, a fast-raiding midfield player in the style of Steve Coppell, was signed for £300,000 from Burnley. The side for the first match was: Jim Arnold, Alan Harper, John Bailey, Derek Mountfield, Mark

Mark Higgins was Kevin Ratcliffe's partner at centre-back and club captain when pelvic injury ended his career in December 1983. He was told he would never play again, but two years later came back to play for Manchester United.

Andy King scores against Aston Villa. He had two spells at Goodison: from 1976 to 1980, and again from 1982 to 1984 before he was allowed to go to Holland.

Higgins, Kevin Richardson, Trevor Steven, Adrian Heath, Graeme Sharp, Andy King, Kevin Sheedy. As the season progressed, Reid and Stevens became regulars as Higgins was injured and temporarily retired, and Harper and King lost their places. Andy Gray was bought to reinforce the forward power and began making appearances from November.

The bright hopes quickly faded, as the side began badly and got worse. By January the team had slumped to 18th in the table. For three months there had been rumblings of 'Kendall out' from the fans and forecasts about the manager's future were in all the tabloids.

The tide turned on 18 January 1984 at an apparently routine Milk Cup tie at Oxford. How Everton scrambled an inglorious draw is described in Chapter 5.

Everton played nine more games without losing from then on, and even then defeat by Aston Villa was in a two-leg Milk Cup semi-final and failed to wipe out Everton's first-leg advantage. By then Goodison was buzzing again. Liverpool were to be the Milk Cup final opponents, and meanwhile were due

The homecoming in 1984. Everton players display the FA Cup to their fans from an open-topped bus in a triumphant tour of the city.

at Goodison on 3 March 1984. A crowd of old-time proportions, 51,245, watched a 1–1 draw. Before they lost again Everton were in the FA Cup semi-final. Although the Milk Cup final was lost to Liverpool over two exciting games, as described in Chapter 5, compensation was that receipts topped £1 million.

Southampton were the FA Cup semi-final opponents, and were beaten 1–0 by an Adrian Heath goal at Highbury. The story of how Watford were beaten 2–0 at Wembley is also told in Chapter 5.

The impetus of the Cup runs lifted the side to seventh in the First Division. In a little more than two months, one of the unhappiest clubs in the country had been transformed into one with pride again. An own-goal by an opponent had been instrumental in effecting the change.

Kendall, on his way to becoming the sort of manager that Spanish clubs pay a fortune for, could so easily have joined Bingham and Lee in the ranks of those who failed to lift Everton back to their proper place.

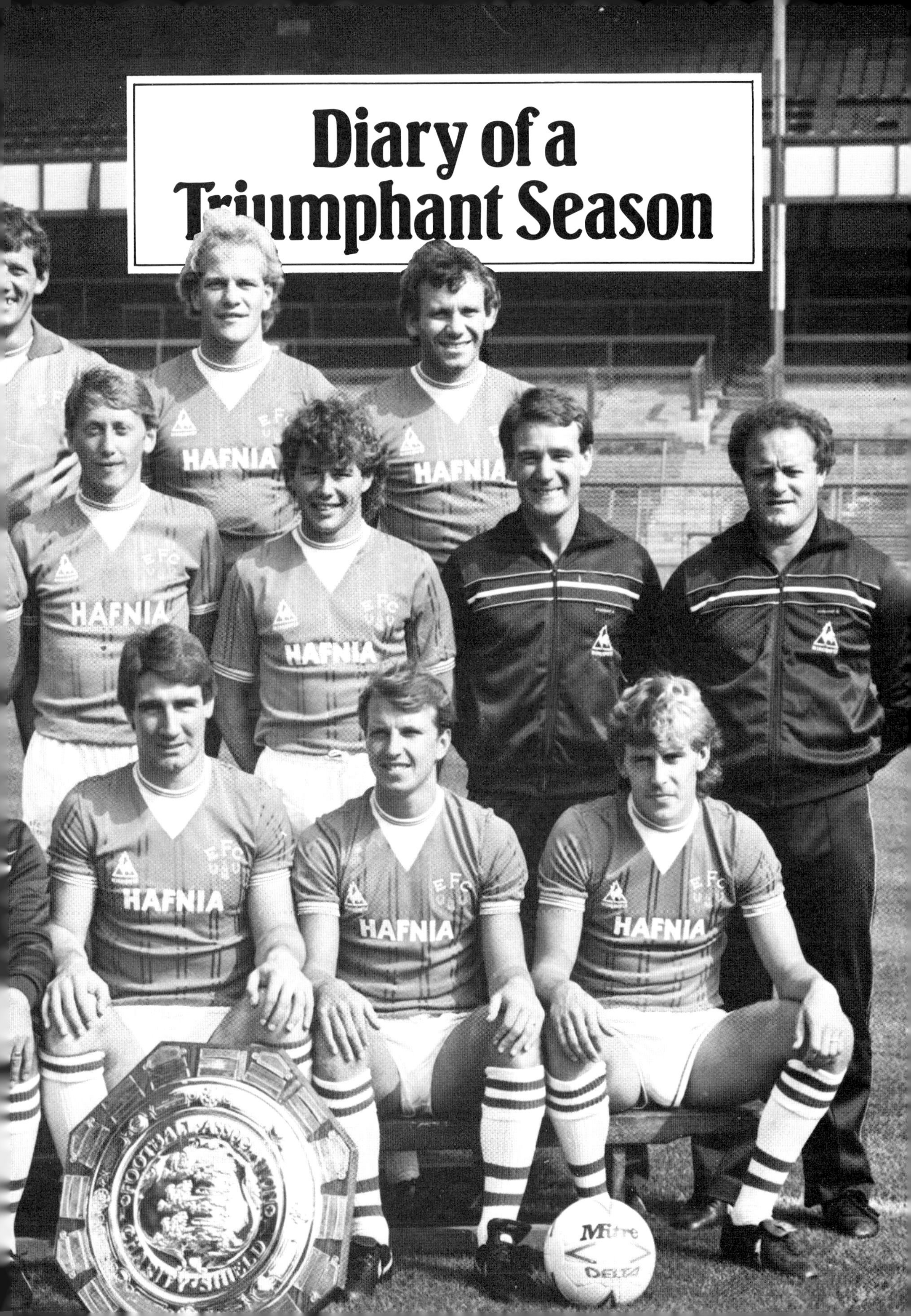
Diary of a
Triumphant Season

Paul Bracewell joined Everton in the week they won the Cup final, and made his first appearance for the Blues in the Charity Shield victory at Wembley.

The victorious FA Cup final at Wembley was Everton's 61st and last match of the 1983–84 season. From the beginning of January 1984 the side had played 35 games and had lost only five. From the depression of 1983, a squad had emerged which looked capable of challenging for further honours. In the summer of 1984 the new season started with optimism in the corridors and offices of Goodison.

The FA Cup final team was available, and had been strengthened. Paul Bracewell had been signed from Sunderland at the time of the Cup final, and gave more options to the midfield. Kevin Sheedy was also waiting in the wings to reclaim his place. On the other hand Andy King, after 242 appearances up to the final League game of the previous season, had been allowed to go.

The first match was the Charity Shield game at Wembley, a continuation of the previous season's Milk Cup final, and an all-Merseyside affair. Bracewell came into the side immediately, thus making his debut for the Blues at Wembley. He took the place of Andy Gray – otherwise the team was the Cup final side: Southall, Stevens, Bailey, Ratcliffe, Mountfield, Reid, Steven, Heath, Sharp, Bracewell, Richardson.

For the first time in ten years Wembley was filled for the Charity Shield. In contrast to the rain of the previous year's Milk Cup final, the day was hot and sticky. The red and blue favours mingled as amicably as before on the terraces and the game was fought with the same commitment on the field – after all, it was Everton and Liverpool.

Everton's younger side began with skill and speed, and for most of the first half overran Liverpool. Grobbelaar, Lawrenson and the rest had to be at their most alert to keep the scoresheet blank at half-time.

Early in the second half Liverpool brought on their new forward signing, Paul Walsh, but in the 56th minute Everton took the lead. Sharp, who had proved slippery from the start, got through and advanced into the area. Grobbelaar rushed out and blocked the shot, but Sharp seized on the rebound and slid it past him. This time Hansen had got back to clear from the line, but as Grobbelaar rushed back, too, the ball struck his shin and went in. It was an unfortunate Grobbelaar own-goal.

Liverpool were unable to reply, and Everton had beaten their rivals in a showpiece match. 'We beat the best today, and deserved to', said Kendall, no doubt aware that soon Everton might be 'the best'. It was the best possible start to the season.

The first League match was a terrible let-down. Spurs arrived at Goodison without Hoddle or Ardiles, and over 35,000 fans turned up to see the new Blues. For half-an-hour Everton ran around Spurs. When Miller handled after 16 minutes, Heath coolly converted the penalty. Then things went wrong. After 38 minutes Southall was slow advancing out of his goal and Falco toed the ball past him. Three minutes later the ball bounced off Ratcliffe and Clive Allen scored. After seven minutes of the second half Southall's fist only pushed the ball to Allen – he scored again. Four minutes later Chiedozie flicked in with his head, after Ratcliffe had headed on. Gray came on for Richardson, but a 4–1 defeat at home had to be endured. The high hopes had failed at the first hurdle.

West Bromwich Albion away on the Monday offered no relief. Curran came in for Bracewell, but the team looked out of sorts. Albion's Hunt and Thompson headed goals in the 57th and 81st minutes. Another Heath penalty three minutes from time only reduced the margin of defeat.

Chelsea were to play a significant part in Everton's fortunes in this season. Everton met them on a Friday evening in a match televised live. The previous season's Second-Division champions had begun their latest top-flight career with four points from their two games, but they disappointed their fans this night. With Bracewell restored, and playing in an all-grey strip for the TV cameras, Everton grabbed an opportunist goal through Kevin Richardson in the 56th minute, and then contained Chelsea's fight-back, with Stevens clearing off the line near the end.

This victory marked the first of six unbeaten games which moved the Blues up the table to sixth. It was far from convincing at first. A 78th minute goal by Heath was needed to earn a late home point against Ipswich, and it needed two more late goals, by Steven and Sharp, to overtake a first-half lead which lowly Coventry had taken at Goodison.

Curran had been substituted for Richardson in these two games. For the visit to Newcastle United, Sheedy was back in the No. 11 shirt. Newcastle had come up from the Second Division, and after three matches led the table, but a 5–0 defeat at Old Trafford the week before the Everton game exposed their pretensions.

Kevin Sheedy, midfield player, left-wing expert and free-kick specialist, celebrates a goal against Southampton.

On a greasy pitch in drizzling rain, Everton conceded a penalty after 12 minutes, converted by Beardsley. After 25 minutes Sheedy celebrated his return by equalizing from just inside the area. A bad back-pass by Mountfield straight after the second-half kick-off enabled Wharton to collect the ball and restore Newcastle's lead. It was an exciting, full-blooded match, and Everton levelled it again after 52 minutes. Ratcliffe took the ball through and Steven drove it home. Two minutes from the end Gray, playing in this match instead of Sharp, bundled in a corner, and Everton's League run gained momentum.

The next game was the first round, first leg, of the European Cup Winners' Cup, and Everton crossed the Irish Sea to face University College Dublin, a mid-table part-time side celebrating its first-ever honour. Surprisingly, Everton showed little ambition, and both sides seemed happy to settle for a 0–0 draw.

Back in the League, there was another disappointing display against Southampton. A weakened Saints side were two goals down at Goodison after nine minutes to Mountfield and Sharp. Set up for slaughter, Southampton forced a draw with goals just before and after the interval.

In a Milk Cup second-round first-leg tie at Second-Division Sheffield United, goals from Sharp and Mountfield enabled the Blues to equalize twice and come away with a draw. There followed one of the most exciting League matches of the season at Watford, who at that stage were propping up the table. Reilly headed the home side ahead in the 15th minute. But Everton had been looking good, and took the lead in a rush. A delightful move between Steven and Heath allowed the former to accept a backheeled pass and shoot home thrillingly in the 33rd minute. Two minutes later Heath himself scored, and right on half-time he added another when Sharp chested the ball down.

Derek Mountfield, Ratcliffe's partner in the centre of defence. Mountfield scored 10 league goals, often from set pieces.

In the 56th minute Mountfield headed into his own net after a free-kick muddle, but six minutes later Mountfield was causing confusion in the other box, scoring after a corner. Watford climbed back to 4–3 in the 72nd minute when Barnes set up a goal for Callaghan, and a minute later Barnes might have equalized, but Stevens got the ball off the line. Sharp made it 5–3 when a Southall punt eluded the defence, but Callaghan set up a goal for Barnes three minutes from the end. In the excitement of the final minutes, Curran, a second-half substitute for Sheedy, was sent off for swearing at a linesman. Everton won 5–4.

On the following Tuesday Sharp scored against University College Dublin, and Everton progressed, not very gloriously, in Europe. The match was notable, however, because Pat van den Hauwe, just bought from relegated Birmingham City, went straight into the side at left-back, and took over more or less permanently from John Bailey.

Everton lost their next League match 1–0 at Highbury. The goal came from a penalty right on half-time, given on the linesman's urging. Heath was booked in the protests. Arsenal led the table: Everton were comfortably placed at eighth.

Sheffield United were despatched in the second leg of the Milk Cup tie at Goodison 4–0: Mountfield, Bracewell, Sharp and Heath helping themselves. Sharp and Heath scored again in a 2–1 win over Aston Villa, Harper playing in Sheedy's No. 11 shirt, which he retained for the League visit to Anfield.

Over 48,000 saw Everton demonstrate again that they were now a younger and faster side than Liverpool; they also matched them for skill. Three minutes after half-time Sharp scored a brilliant goal, winning the ball and, from the inside-right position well outside the penalty area, firing a dipping shot over Grobbelaar's head into the net. Before this match Alan Irvine had left for Crystal Palace for £50,000, having asked for a transfer.

In mid-week the Blues journeyed to Czechoslovakia and beat Inter Bratislava 1–0 in the second round of their European quest. Harper and Bailey played for Sheedy and van den Hauwe, respectively, and Bracewell was the scorer.

The Blues were now playing at a peak. Back at Goodison Sheedy and van den Hauwe returned and Manchester United were demolished 5–0 (this game is described in Chapter 5). Everton moved over United from fourth to second in the Championship, with Arsenal two points ahead.

Over 40,000 watched this match. Over 50,000 watched the next, which was a Milk Cup third-round match – at Old Trafford. Harper took the No. 11 shirt again, Sheedy having a bad time with injuries hereabouts.

United started aggressively, and took the lead in the 23rd minute. Olsen cleverly found Moses, whose volley across the area was driven by Moran and deflected in by Brazil. Three minutes before half-time Heath was fouled by Hogg, and Sharp equalized from the spot. United's fire blew itself out in the second half, and the match looked like a stalemate until a cross was deflected in the United goalmouth, and the unfortunate Gidman, an ex-Evertonian, headed it over his goalkeeper in attempting to clear. There were only six minutes left. Everton had confirmed their superiority over Manchester United.

On 3 November, three second-half goals from Steven, Sheedy and Heath saw Leicester beaten 3–0 at Goodison and Everton went to the top of the League, Arsenal having lost at Old Trafford. Sharp, Sheedy and Heath scored without reply at Goodison in mid-week to end Inter Bratislava's European ambitions, then Heath scored the only goal at West Ham before the doomed Stoke City visited Goodison and lost 4–0, the admirable Heath notching two more, and Steven and Reid getting the others.

The Milk Cup fourth round came next, and Second-Division Grimsby Town arrived for what was expected to be a slaughter. But goalkeeper Nigel Batch played a blinder, having the share of luck which goalies deserve, defenders made three goal-line clearances, and after 89 minutes Everton led by 19–0, but only in corners. Then Grimsby, having practically earned a replay, won the match. Paul Wilkinson was tripped by Reid, and headed in the free-kick.

A stutter in the League followed this upset. Norwich City, inspired by John Deehan, scored three goals in 10 minutes at Carrow Road. Everton, who were not noticeably the inferior side, came back to 3–2 through Sharp and Sheedy, but Deehan wrapped it up with another.

The next match was a depressing one for the Blues. Wednesday visited Goodison and after seven minutes led through Andy Blair. Ex-Blues Lyons and Varadi were in the Wednesday side, but the exchanges were not too friendly. After 18 minutes a foul by Brian Marwood on Adrian Heath left the Everton player with severely damaged knee ligaments which put him out for the rest of the season. Sharp equalized with a penalty when Blair barged into him in the area after 28 minutes, then just before half-time Marwood was carried off after a tackle by Reid. There was more unpleasantness but no more goals.

Andy Gray took over Heath's shirt for the rest of the season, but the main

Graeme Sharp gets in the magnificent shot which beat Bruce Grobbelaar and Liverpool at Anfield in October and gave Everton belief in themselves.

impact he made on the visit to Queens Park Rangers was to challenge so vigorously that a fist-fight started in midfield. Pat van den Hauwe and Simon Stainrod were sent off, and Gray was booked; there were no goals. Everton remained top of the League because Manchester United and Arsenal both lost.

Everton produced a Championship performance against Nottingham Forest in their next match, winning 5–0, Sharp (2), Sheedy, Steven and Reid scoring. Forest ended with nine men: one injured, one sent off.

Ironically, having hit form at last, the Blues were toppled from the leadership the following week when Chelsea visited Goodison and won 4–3. Gordon Davies, who was not to stay long at Chelsea, was their hero. He opened the scoring with a neat header after 10 minutes. Bracewell equalized after 35 minutes with a cross-shot, but Davies restored Chelsea's lead for half-time. After 61 minutes Pat Nevin beat four defenders and laid on another for Colin Pates. Eight minutes later Joe McLaughlin tangled with Andy Gray and Sharp reduced the arrears with a penalty. Nevin once more nipped through to give Davies his hat-trick. Two minutes from the end McLaughlin handled and Sharp scored his second penalty, but Everton had been easily beaten. They dropped to third behind Spurs and Manchester United, but the significance of this defeat was that it was the last for 28 games.

Two away games, at Sunderland and Ipswich, were won 2–0 and 2–1, Mountfield scoring both goals in the first game, and Sharp doing the same in the second. Then Luton Town were beaten 2–0 at home, Steven this time scoring both goals.

It was now the New Year, and the FA Cup competition began for the first two divisions. Everton were drawn at Leeds in the third round. The match was chosen by the BBC for its live Friday evening transmission on 4 January. A

Preceding pages As a back-four player, Derek Mountfield does more than his share of causing chaos in opponents' goal-mouths, and here he has even Peter Shilton under pressure.

young Leeds side fought hard but were no match for a strong-tackling Everton who, although they won only 2–0, were not in danger. In the 40th minute Andy Linighan handled in the area, and Leeds' hopes virtually disappeared as Sharp stroked home the penalty. Leeds battled for a draw, but five minutes from the end Sheedy's fierce free-kick struck the bar, the ball shot up in the air, and when Gray rose highest to nod it into space, Sheedy was there to crack it back into the net.

Newcastle visited Goodison in the League on the following Saturday, and were overrun. Sharp, Mountfield and Sheedy (2) scored without reply, and because Spurs were held to a draw at Queens Park Rangers, Everton went to the top of the table again.

The fourth round of the FA Cup brought Doncaster Rovers to Goodison. There was no giant-killing, as Steven and Stevens scored before half-time to wrap it up.

Another home game followed, with Watford, reviving memories of the nine-goal match at Vicarage Road. This time there was a blank score-sheet till half-time, then Stevens (2), Sheedy and Steven netted without reply.

The numbered marbles in the little black bag were kind to Everton once more with another home draw against comparatively weak opposition in the fifth round of the FA Cup: non-League Telford United did well to shut Everton out for more than an hour, but then the 'S' men did the trick again: Stevens, Sheedy (penalty) and Steven won the match 3–0. These three players had scored the last eleven goals – and the season's leading scorer was another 'S': Sharp.

The Blues had to travel to Leicester for the next League game. Gray scored first, and, when Leicester equalized, scored the winner within a minute. A visit to Old Trafford failed to bring to Manchester United revenge for their earlier defeats, but an all-action match was enjoyed by over 51,000 fans. Jesper Olsen had a brilliant game, and United should have taken the lead after four minutes, when his progress into the area was abruptly and illegally halted by Stevens; Strachan's soft penalty was saved easily by Southall. Van den Hauwe and Reid, together with Whiteside and Hughes, earned the referee's displeasure, and a further foul by Reid achieved a booking. Stevens, as if annoyed with Strachan for missing the penalty, almost scored an own-goal, then in the 36th minute United did score, when Olsen drilled home a beauty. Five minutes later Steven's corner was knocked on by Curran, in the side because of injury to Sharp, and Mountfield equalized with a header.

Despite Olsen's raids, Everton were the better side in the second half and six minutes from the end might have won when Albiston pushed Steven in the area. Sheedy took the spot kick in Sharp's absence but Gary Bailey dived and pushed the shot away for a corner. The draw kept Everton two points clear of Spurs, with a gap developing thereafter.

The Cup Winners' Cup resumed in March, and Everton faced Fortuna Sittard, of Holland, at Goodison in the first leg of the quarter-final. Impatient in the first half, Everton failed to score, but Andy Gray scored a hat-trick after the interval to give the Blues a comfortable three-goal cushion for the away leg.

Everton were at home again in the sixth round of the FA Cup – at least in Ipswich they faced opposition of their own standard. Everton began brightly and had already had two efforts disallowed before Sheedy curled a free-kick round the wall after five minutes to put them ahead. After a quarter of an hour, however, Kevin Wilson shot from 25 yards and Southall missed it – he was entitled to one error having kept brilliantly all season. After 31 minutes it was a question of 'Wherefore art thou, Southall?' as Romeo Zondervan from Surinam hooked in a beautiful volley.

As the second half progressed Everton went for the equalizer rather

Kevin Richardson made 14 League appearances plus one as substitute – just enough for a Championship medal – in 1984–85.

Above *Kevin Ratcliffe, the team captain in 1984–85 (Mark Higgins was club captain but could not play).*

robustly. Tempers became frayed and Sheedy and three Ipswich players were booked: Butcher, Gates and McCall. Thirteen minutes from the end McCall was sent off, but the 10 men of Ipswich appeared capable of surviving the constant Everton pressure until at last van den Hauwe centred for Mountfield to slide home. Everton could regard this result as the little bit of luck which sides need to get to Wembley.

There was a very sad postscript to the match, however, when Harry Catterick, manager of the last Championship side in 1970, died in the directors' box as the match finished.

Sharp's absence, together with the long one of Heath, meant Everton had played four matches without their two principal strikers, and well though Gray and Curran deputized, Howard Kendall decided to buy another striker. Paul Wilkinson, Grimsby's England Under-21 international, whose goal at Goodison had removed the Blues from the Milk Cup in November, now came to Goodison to join the playing staff for a fee of £250,000.

Sharp was back for the FA Cup replay at Ipswich, but Sheedy was out through injury, Harper deputizing. Ipswich pressed but Steven came closest with a shot off the bar. With less than a quarter of an hour to play and the match still undecided, an awkwardly bouncing ball struck Russell Osman's hand in the Ipswich 18-yard box. The referee gave a penalty and Sharp beat the reserve goalkeeper, Mark Grew, who got a touch but just failed to stop the shot. Five minutes from the end Steve McCall's shot came back off a post and Ipswich knew that it was Everton who were destined to go into the semi-final.

Back in the League Aston Villa were held 1–1 at Villa Park, Kevin Richardson

deputizing for Reid and scoring a goal. Then it was off to Holland, where Reid returned to the side and grabbed the winning goal. So did Sharp in a 2–0 win – Fortuna Sittard were beaten 5–0 on aggregate. Harper, Richardson and Curran all played, and Bob Wakenshaw came on for Ratcliffe.

There followed a run of Championship games. Arsenal were beaten 2–0 at Goodison, Gray and Sharp scoring, and then Southampton were beaten 2–1 at the Dell. Kevin Richardson, now wearing the No. 11 shirt, scored twice in three minutes just after half-time: Southampton's consolation effort came in injury time. Paul Wilkinson made his first appearance in this game as a substitute for Sharp.

A Wednesday-evening match at Tottenham was crucial to the Championship. Spurs needed to win it to join Everton on points at the top of the table. The goal differences would have been similar, too.

Sheedy was back, and the side was the strongest possible, given Heath's continued absence. After 10 minutes, one of Southall's long punts out of the area was headed by Paul Miller to Gray, who beat Ray Clemence from just inside the area. Later Gray limped off and Harper replaced him. After 61 minutes Steven scored a very cool goal, dispossessing Mark Bowen and swerving round Clemence before tapping the ball home. Seventeen minutes from time Graham Roberts smashed home a 25-yard special, and Spurs pressed hard for an equalizer to keep their Championship hopes alive. There were three minutes left when a Hoddle centre was met perfectly by Mark Falco, but Southall made a superb point-blank save. Spurs dropped six points adrift, and Everton looked like Champions-elect.

Above *The striker in reserve. Kendall paid Grimsby Town £250,000 for Paul Wilkinson before the transfer deadline in 1985 and he played four matches at the end of the season.*

Left *A typical Andy Gray effort – diving in where it is most dangerous. This header earned the second goal in his hat-trick against Fortuna Sittard of Holland in the first leg of the Cup Winners' Cup quarter-final at Goodison.*

There were no mistakes made at Goodison – Sunderland were well beaten 4–1, Gray (2) and Steven being the scorers and Sunderland contributing an own-goal.

Four days later the team flew to Munich to meet Bayern in the Cup Winners' Cup semi-final, first leg. Richardson and Harper played for the injured Sheedy and Gray in front of 70,000 spectators. Everton played a perfect away leg, defending brilliantly, particularly through van den Hauwe and Ratcliffe, and doing enough up front to keep Bayern stretched. A 0–0 draw was regarded as a distinct success.

Then it was the FA Cup semi-final at Villa Park. Luton, from the lower reaches of the First Division, provided unexpectedly stern opposition. Gray and Sheedy returned after injury. Luton were the better side in the first half, and were full value for the lead they took in the 36th minute, when Ricky Hill drove a long shot in via a post. In the second half Bracewell also hit the post, but the ball rebounded into play. Luton began to settle down to defend their lead, and seemed likely to do so successfully, but five minutes from time were a little unlucky to concede a free-kick just outside the area. Sheedy produced one of his best efforts, and although Les Sealey touched the ball, he could not stop the equalizer.

The goal shook Luton psychologically as their players were already looking forward to an unexpected appearance at Wembley. It lifted Everton, and six minutes from the end of extra-time they won another free-kick, and this time Mountfield met another well-placed ball from Sheedy and headed the winner. Everton were at Wembley, and could not complain about their luck in the FA Cup.

Back at Goodison in the League, West Bromwich Albion were beaten 4–1, with Ian Atkins taking a central defensive role in Mountfield's place, and scoring after two minutes. Sharp (2, one a penalty) and Sheedy scored the others. Stoke City were then beaten 2–0 at home, Sharp and Sheedy scoring.

Now it was the second leg of the Cup Winners' Cup semi-final, and Bayern Munich came to Goodison only to lose in a pulsating evening of football (the match is described in Chapter 5). Everton were now in two cup finals and were a comfortable 10 points clear in the Championship (with two games in hand). A unique treble was very much a possibility.

The Championship turned out to be no problem. Norwich were beaten 3–0 at home (Mountfield, Steven and Bracewell getting on the scoresheet), and Sheffield Wednesday 1–0 away (Gray). When Queens Park Rangers arrived at Goodison on Bank Holiday Monday, 6 May, only one point was needed to wrap up the title, and 50,514 turned up to see them do it. Mountfield scored after 25 minutes, and when Sharp added a second with eight minutes left, the celebrations could really begin.

The team had now gone 26 games without defeat and had won nine League games running. They made it 10 the following Wednesday, when West Ham United were beaten 3–0 at Goodison, Gray and Mountfield (2) scoring. On this night, the Championship trophy was brought across Stanley Park from Anfield and handed to the Blues.

At last the team lost after a 28-match undefeated run, when they went down 1–0 at Nottingham Forest. It was not surprising that, with two cup finals looming and the Championship won, there was a relaxation.

The first final was the European Cup Winners' Cup final, in which Rapid Vienna were overcome 3–1 in Rotterdam, as described in Chapter 5.

The second was the FA Cup final which, if won, would make Everton the fifth team to achieve the legendary 'double' of Cup and Championship. Their opponents were Manchester United, whom Everton had already beaten twice during the season.

The players who followed Howard Kendall on to the pitch at Wembley were: Southall, Stevens, van den Hauwe, Ratcliffe, Mountfield, Reid, Steven, Sharp, Gray, Bracewell and Sheedy.

Reid hit a post for Everton early on, and then tackled Mark Hughes when he looked threatening. But somehow the match failed to take off in the muggy atmosphere. Everton at last seemed weary after their long season. They had been on a high only three days earlier in Rotterdam. It was their 60th match of the season – as it was for United.

In the second half Southall made a brilliant save from the advancing Whiteside but, despite the physical effort, a mental torpor had settled on the match. The referee stirred it up somewhat 13 minutes from the end, however, by sending off Kevin Moran for a foul on Reid, a decision which did not meet with a lot of approval in the press or among either camp. This reverse seemed to inspire United into more cohesive action, while Everton appeared unable to think of a way of exploiting their superior numbers.

Extra-time came, and five minutes into the second period Norman Whiteside was sent away up the right wing. With defenders hurrying back and attackers wearily trying to make ground for the expected cross, Whiteside decided to swing a left-foot shot across the face of the goal. It beat Southall's dive and curled in beautifully at the foot of the far post. It was a brilliant individual goal to redeem a somewhat mechanical match.

The goal which made almost certain of the Championship. Derek Mountfield turns away after putting Everton in front against Queens Park Rangers at Goodison Park on 6 May 1985.

Everton did not seem unduly disappointed and, after all, it had been a magnificent season – not that it was over. There were still three League games to complete – the first at Goodison against Liverpool. The biggest home crowd of the season (51,045) came to see their heroes, despite the Cup final defeat. Everton fielded a strange side, with Bailey, Richardson, Harper, Wilkinson and Atkins playing. The match was hotly contested. John Wark missed a penalty for Liverpool before Wilkinson scored the only goal. It marked Everton's first League double over Liverpool since 1964–65. Not all the fans were happy with the club, however. There was a demonstration against the new shirts with their broad white band from shoulder to shoulder. It was a pity that, in their moment of triumph, the club should dilute the famous blue colours.

A visit to Coventry ended in a 4–1 defeat, equalling the biggest of the

Despite beating Manchester United 5–0 earlier in the season, Everton lost 1–0 to them in the FA Cup final. Pat van den Hauwe gets in a shot which beats Gary Bailey but goes over the bar. Paul McGrath and Norman Whiteside look on.

season, suffered against Spurs on the first day. The win saved Coventry from relegation. The last match was at Luton, where only Southall and van den Hauwe of the Cup final side played. Luton's 2–0 win hardly compensated them for the semi-final defeat.

So ended the most successful season in Everton's history. 'Player of the Year' Southall was ever-present, Steven and Ratcliffe missed only two games each, Stevens and Mountfield five, Reid and Bracewell six, Sharp eight. Only six teams failed to include either Heath or his substitute Gray. Van den Hauwe missed only five games from his introduction into the side. Sheedy suffered most from injury, but played in exactly two-thirds of the 63 matches. Bailey, Curran and Harper were the main reserves. These were the players who made Everton great again.

So near yet so far in 1985–86. After their triumphant season in 1984–85, Everton began the next with one major regret. Qualified for the European Cup, they were denied the chance to follow up their first European success by the ban on English clubs' participation, following the tragedy instigated by Liverpool supporters at the Heysel Stadium, Brussels, before the previous season's European Cup final.

On the other hand the acquisition of the England striker, Gary Lineker, from Leicester City promised to strengthen an already strong attack, and a season of thrilling football, goals, and more domestic trophies was confidently expected.

The hopes looked justified in the Charity Shield match, a re-run of the Cup final, but this time with the Blues convincing 2–0 winners. Fielding their strongest side, Everton galloped round Manchester United in the sunshine, and their day was complete when 15 minutes from the end Adrian Heath returned after his long absence with injury and promptly slotted in the second goal. It was a pattern he was to repeat throughout the season.

However, it was United who immediately shot into the Championship lead, winning their first 10 games and after a third of the season standing 10 points clear and looking uncatchable.

Everton began their League programme at Leicester, and lost 3–1, with Lineker's replacement, Bright, scoring twice. Their start was as uneasy as the previous year's, but a Lineker hat-trick against doomed Birmingham promised better things, and soon the team had climbed to second place. Sharp was dropped for the visit of Luton, came on as substitute, scored, and thereafter was Lineker's regular partner in a striking duo that was to prove the most lethal in the First Division. Heath became a frequent substitute.

Liverpool won 3–2 at Goodison, with Steve McMahon, a recent Evertonian, notching the third. Defeat by 2–1 at Chelsea, where Southall was sent off to his obvious displeasure, dropped the Blues to sixth, and another 2–1 defeat at West Ham two weeks later dropped them to seventh. On the day Manchester United lost their first game, Everton beat Arsenal 6–1, but were still 14 points behind.

In December, the Blues were eliminated from the Milk Cup. A 2–2 draw at Stamford Bridge was followed by a 2–1 defeat by 10 Chelsea men at Goodison. By the end of the year, though, Everton had advanced to third in the table, behind Manchester United (who were declining) and Chelsea. On 2 February, a 1–0 win over Spurs took Everton to the top.

On the softer grounds, the Blues' game became stronger. A 2–0 victory at Anfield on 23 February emphasized their title aspirations, and a recovery from two down to draw at Luton in the FA Cup quarter-final emphasized that they had lost none of their fighting qualities. Substitute Heath got the equalizer.

Liverpool became the challengers in the League but with a point or two and a game or two in hand throughout March, the Blues appeared to have the situation under control. Moreover, Luton in the replay, and Sheffield Wednesday in the semi-final (after extra-time), were despatched from the FA Cup, and Everton and Liverpool were engaged in a struggle for supremacy which could bring the Cup and League double to either. Everton were favourites, despite a sad injury to Neville Southall while playing for Wales on 26 March. Torn ankle ligaments put him out for the season, but Bobby Mimms was to prove an excellent substitute.

Not until 30 April did Everton make their one slip in the League, and ironically it came at Oxford, where the big revival had begun just over two years earlier in a Milk Cup match. Coincidentally, Oxford had just won the Milk Cup themselves, but were fighting relegation. Two minutes from the end of an evenly fought game, Oxford scored (it was the first goal Mimms

Preceding pages
Bruce Grobbelaar, Liverpool's eccentric goalkeeper, reaches high above Graeme Sharp's head. The Country's top goalscorer Gary Lineker looks on. Steve Nicol and Ronnie Whelan are the two Liverpool defenders.

conceded – in his seventh match) and despite two minutes of frenetic Everton pressure, three points were lost. Liverpool, meanwhile, refused to drop a single point over their last games, and Everton were relegated to second place in the League.

The Cup final was the last chance of an honour. The Wembley side was: Mimms, Stevens, van den Hauwe, Ratcliffe, Mountfield, Reid, Steven, Lineker, Sharp, Bracewell, Sheedy. Heath was substitute.

Everton played impressively in the first half, had a good claim for a penalty rejected (by referee Robinson, who had also refused them one in the Milk Cup final two years earlier), but still led from a good goal by Lineker, who beat Grobbelaar at the second attempt after a defence-splitting ball from Reid. Everton were completely on top at the beginning of the second half, and the Liverpool defence was forced into all kinds or errors, with Sheedy going close twice. However, it was a Gary Stevens error that finally was punished, with Rush scoring an equalizer against the run of play. The Blues did not lose their composure, and Sharp almost restored the lead with a header that Grobbelaar, caught out of position, needed all his athleticism to push over the bar.

Almost immediatley Craig Johnston was through to put Liverpool ahead, and the bold replacement of Stevens by an extra forward, Heath, merely unbalanced Everton and Rush subsequently added a third.

So instead of the 'Double' Everton had won nothing. A marvellous season up to the end of April had crashed in 11 days. As Howard Kendall said: 'It's shattering when you think of who won the Double'.

Kevin Ratcliffe, the captain of Wales, and Ian Rush, the Welsh centre-forward, in the fiercest football opposition one can get: Everton v. Liverpool.

Famous Evertonians

This section contains biographies of players who made over 250 League appearances for the Blues, or were famous internationals, or who otherwise demand inclusion.

Walter Abbott. He was bought from Small Heath (now Birmingham) after the 1898–99 season, part of the transfer fee being a benefit match which Everton played at Small Heath. Abbott played at inside-right and was the Midland League's top scorer, but he failed as a forward at Everton, and was soon switched to left-half in the reserves. There his energy and enthusiasm made him an inspirational midfield dynamo, and he became a regular for almost nine seasons, chalking up nearly 300 appearances altogether and frequently scoring goals. He played once for England, and twice for Everton in the Cup final, including the famous victory over Newcastle in 1906. In 1908 he went to Burnley, then back to Birmingham.

John Bailey. Born in Liverpool on April Fools' Day, 1957, he signed for Everton from Blackburn Rovers, where he had been an apprentice, in the summer of 1979 for £300,000. A fast and adventurous full-back, he was Everton's only ever-present in his first season, and became a member of England's B squad. Although suffering occasional injury, he was a regular until 1983–84, when he won an FA Cup winners' medal in the 2–0 defeat of Watford, and also played in the Milk Cup final. He lost his place the following season to Pat van den Hauwe, but has remained in the squad to the end of the season.

Alan Ball. An indefatigable footballer, he achieved immortality in the 1966 World Cup final, when he seemed to cover every inch of the pitch and in extra-time had the energy to chase the ball down the wing and cross for Hurst to score the goal which gave England victory.

Ball was originally turned down by Bolton, his local side, because they said he was too small, but he signed for Blackpool as an apprentice, making his First-Division debut in 1962. Three days before his 20th birthday, in 1965, he played for England. After his World Cup triumph, while still just 21, he joined Everton for a then-record British fee of £110,000. Ball was an inside-forward, usually on the right, who in his younger days took on an attacking winger's role and in his later days that of a polished midfielder. He stood only 5ft 6in. (1.68m) tall and weighed 10st 5lb (67.9kg), but was so combative that he was often accused of having a fiery temper. Perhaps his red hair did not help his cause. Certainly there was never a more competitive player, and he was captain of many sides he played for, including Everton and, briefly, England.

At Goodison Ball formed a legendary midfield partnership with Howard Kendall and Colin Harvey in the late 1960s. The side fought each season for League and FA Cup, and although the Cup final was lost in 1968, the Championship arrived in 1970. Then things went sour, and after two seasons in mid-table, Catterick sold Ball to Arsenal for another record fee – £220,000. Ball played 249 times for Everton and scored 78 goals. After Arsenal he went to Southampton, then into management at Blackpool and Portsmouth. His last match was for Southampton against Everton in 1982. In all he won 72 caps for England.

Walter Balmer. He was a full-back who played 331 games in 12 seasons for Everton around the turn of the century. He was born in Liverpool, and his brother and nephew were also to turn out for Everton. A solid full-back, Balmer played once for England in 1905, and in 1906 and 1907 he played for Everton in the Cup final, on the first occasion as a winner.

Local-born dressing-room joker John Bailey was the irrepressible enthusiastic left-back for five seasons but lost his place early in 1984–85 when Pat van den Hauwe arrived.

Preceding pages Alex Young, the 'Golden Vision', showing the FA Cup to the fans at Wembley after the defeat of Sheffield Wednesday in 1966.

John Bell.   Another Evertonian whose career spanned the 19th and 20th centuries. A Scotsman, he won a Championship medal with Dumbarton in 1891–92 before joining Everton the following year, making just three appearances at the end of his first season at Goodison Park. He was to miss honours with his new club, twice League runners-up and beaten Cup finalists before he left in 1897–98. A brilliant dribbler on the left wing, he was outstanding in the 1897 Cup final, scoring an individual goal in the 3–2 defeat by Aston Villa. He returned to Everton for two seasons in 1901. He won 10 Scottish caps, three of them while with Everton.

Billy Bingham.   This quietly spoken Irishman played from 1950 to 1964, for Sunderland, Luton, Everton and Port Vale. Born in Belfast in 1931, he was a very tricky outside-right who played 56 times for Northern Ireland, which at the time equalled Danny Blanchflower's record for his country. He spent three seasons at Goodison, and was a member of the Championship-winning side in 1962–63. He moved on to Port Vale after this season, and retired when he broke his leg two years later. He returned to Goodison as manager from 1973 to 1977, and in the 1980s managed Northern Ireland.

Paul Bracewell.   He joined Everton in May 1984, in the week when Everton won the FA Cup. He had been at Sunderland for only one season, having previously been a team-mate of Adrian Heath at Stoke, where he was born in 1962. His first match for Everton was the Charity Shield game in 1984–85. Bracewell immediately took over the No. 10 shirt, and established a midfield partnership with Peter Reid that helped the Blues through to their Championship and Cup-Winners' Cup successes. He is a thoughtful player whose strengths lie in his positional play and accuracy in passing. The England manager soon recognized his talent, and he made his international debut on the summer tour to Mexico in 1985. He is likely to win many honours with club and country.

The new lean and hungry look of Paul Bracewell. The long hair and plumper features of the May 1984 signing seem to have disappeared with the effort of winning the Championship.

Cliff Britton.   Bought from Bristol Rovers in 1930 as a half-back, he had a strange career. He made 10 appearances while the team won the Second Division, but he was considered so frail that the following season he was moved to outside-right in the reserves, and did not play at all for the first team, which continued in successful vein and won the Championship. However, the following year he was back at right-half in the sixth match of the season and missed only one more as Everton took the FA Cup. He developed into a very cultured and constructive half-back, and soon made the first of nine appearances for England. He was decidedly unlucky not to win a Championship medal, as Joe Mercer took his place when Everton won the title again in 1938–39. Yet he was still a good player, and with Mercer and Stan Cullis formed a famous England wartime half-back line, when all three were stationed at Aldershot, for whom they played.

Edgar Chadwick.   One of the great players of the 1890s, he was with the two Blackburn clubs, Rovers and Olympic, before joining Everton in 1888, in time for the first Football League season. He was Everton's only ever-present, and did not miss a League game until nearly the end of the fourth season. By this time Everton had won their first Championship. He was unlucky in Cup finals, twice being on the losing side, and when he left Goodison in 1899 for Southern League Southampton, he was on the losing side again in 1902. A small man, he was a brilliant inside-left, who was picked seven times for England. He made exactly 300 appearances for Everton and scored 110 goals.

Sam Chedgzoy.   He also played exactly 300 times for Everton. He made his debut on Boxing Day 1910, but his first full season was 1914–15 when Everton won their second Championship. Chedgzoy was a very clever outside-right who was picked for England immediately after the First World War and went on to win eight caps. Perhaps his most famous feat occurred in the 1924–25 season when he exploited the rule that goals could be scored direct from a corner by dribbling the ball in against Spurs. The goal was disallowed, but it was decided after the match that it was within the rules and the law was subsequently changed. Chedgzoy retired after the 1925–26 season and went to America.

Dave Clements.   He had been a Northern Ireland international for nearly 10 years when Billy Bingham signed him from Sheffield Wednesday in September 1973. With Wednesday and Coventry he was brilliant at full-back or in midfield, where he shone in his two-and-a-bit years with Everton. Clements was captain, and towards the end of the 1974–75 season was appointed Northern Ireland player-manager. He left Everton during the following season and joined New York Cosmos, losing his managing job but bringing his total of caps to 48.

Bobby Collins.   A Glaswegian, he was the star player who got away. Born in 1931, he was spotted in junior football and joined Everton, but returned north feeling homesick to sign for Celtic. A brilliant inside-forward, he stood only 5ft 4in. (1.63m) tall and weighed 10st 3lb (64.9kg). He was a midfield player who organized his attack, and won the first of his caps when only 20. He rejoined Everton for £25,000 in 1958 and continued playing brilliantly, scoring 48 goals in 147 games, before Harry Catterick sold him to Second-Division Leeds United in 1962. It proved an inspired move for Collins, who was a leading light in the revival of the Yorkshire club. He became a coach and manager after his retirement.

Billy Cook.   He preceded Collins from Celtic to Everton – in 1932. He was a

Brilliant winger Sam Chedgzoy played for the same local side as Joe Mercer's father. His son, another Sam, also joined Everton, but was not successful. Sam senior was an Everton player for 15 years.

determined full-back, who won a Scottish Cup winners' medal in 1931, and an English one with Everton in 1933, not to mention 15 Northern Ireland caps. He also won a Championship medal in 1938–39, his last season at Goodison. Cook was truly international in outlook, because after the war he joined a Welsh club, Wrexham, and after his retirement coached in Peru and Norway before returning home to manage Wigan.

Warney Cresswell.   An innovator, he was a right-back who brought science and anticipation to the position. That he was not universally copied is shown by the fact that Alf Ramsey earned a similar reputation for classy full-back play some 20 years later. Cresswell joined Everton from Sunderland, who had paid South Shields a record £5500 for him in 1922. He arrived at Goodison towards the end of the 1926–27 season to help in the fight against relegation – successfully, as Everton finished 20th. He was made captain, and the following season Everton won a glorious Championship. Not a tall man at 5ft 9½in. (1.77m), the slight and fair-haired Cresswell was not a strong tackler, and succeeded by positional play and speed. He was a good organizer of the defence and won seven England caps. He spent 10 seasons at Goodison, making over 300 appearances, including one season in the Second Division (which Everton won). He won a second Championship medal in 1931–32 and the following season a Cup winners' medal.

Dai Davies.   A great goalkeeper who won 52 caps for Wales, he somehow failed to establish himself fully at Goodison. He arrived in December 1970 from Swansea City and played two games that season, but failed to replace Gordon West, and when Everton paid a record fee for David Lawson in 1972 Davies went back to Swansea on loan. From 1974 to 1977 he made 92 appearances for the Blues, but then was sold cheaply to Wrexham, although he continued to play for Wales for a further six years.

Dixie Dean.   Unquestionably he is Everton's most famous player. Born in 1907 in Birkenhead, he was christened William Ralph, became known to his friends as Bill, and always hated the nickname Dixie. He was building a big reputation as an 18-year-old goalscoring centre-forward with Tranmere Rovers when Everton signed him for £3000 on 16 March 1925. He played in seven matches that season and was dropped for the last two. He did not start the 1925–26 season, but seven goals in a reserve match returned him to the League team in the fifth match of the season – he ended with 32 goals and the legend had begun.

But it was not plain sailing – in the close season he had a dreadful motorcycle accident in North Wales. His skull and jaw were fractured, and he

Possibly the greatest goalscorer in football history. Dixie Dean not only scored 377 goals for Everton, he also scored 18 goals for England – in only 16 appearances.

was not expected to live. He was unconscious for three days and metal plates were inserted into his jaw until the bones knitted. Later on, when the power of his heading was so lethal, the story grew that a metal plate was in his forehead – a myth, of course. Doctors said he would never play again. Four-and-a-half months later he was back with a goal and Everton, who without him had won only one of their first 13 games, revived sufficiently to avoid relegation.

The following season was the great Championship one, and Dean's record of 60 League goals, which is still unbeaten. Including international and representative games, and all Everton's charity and summer tour games, Dean scored exactly 100 goals that season.

Dean won another Championship medal in 1932 and a Cup winners' medal in 1933, when he captained Everton at Wembley. He left Everton in March 1938. In the League and Cup he made 431 appearances and scored 377 goals, a remarkable ratio. He played 16 times for England and scored 18 goals. He is regarded still as the best-ever header of the ball. The Everton historian, Thomas Keates, wrote in 1929: 'Ordinary players butt the ball with the crown of their heads and it usually goes over the bar. Dean artistically glides it downwards with the side of his head. In this respect he excels every other famous centre-forward.' In other words, Dean perfected the art of heading.

After retirement Dean took a pub, and remained a much-loved figure on Merseyside. He had to have a leg amputated in 1976 and died in 1980 – at Goodison Park, after watching the Everton–Liverpool match.

Martin Dobson.   Britain's most expensive footballer at the time, he joined Everton from Burnley for £300,000 in 1974. A midfielder who had been converted from a forward, he was a strong, polished performer who won five England caps. He missed few games in five seasons at Goodison, and was a steadying influence in a period of comings and goings. It was a surprise when he himself returned to Burnley for £100,000 in 1979, never having quite fulfilled his potential.

Jimmy Dunn.   One of those players who have delighted the Goodison fans over the years, he was an inside-forward of outstanding skill, pace and invention. His main claim to fame is that he was one of the Wembley Wizards, the Scottish team that demolished England 5–1 in 1928. None of the forwards was over 5ft 7in. (1.70m) tall, hence their other name, the Wee Blue Devils. Dunn joined Everton from Hibs soon afterwards, and left seven years later in 1935, disappointingly without ever getting in more than 33 games in a season. He won a Championship medal in 1931–32 and the following season scored in the Cup final win over Manchester City.

Tommy Eglington.   He missed few games for Everton in the 11 years after the Second World War, making 428 appearances in all and scoring 82 goals. He and Peter Farrell were signed from Shamrock Rovers for £10,000 in 1946 – an outstanding bargain. He was a complete outside-left who once scored five goals in a match – against Doncaster in the Second Division in 1952. His speed and trickery earned him 24 caps for the Republic of Ireland and another six for Northern Ireland. He was in the Republic's team which beat England 2–0 at Goodison Park in 1949 – England's first-ever defeat at home by a 'foreign' side. In 1957 he left Everton for Tranmere, playing nearly 200 games for them before returning to Dublin.

Peter Farrell.   His career coincided with that of his friend Tommy Eglington. They arrived together from Shamrock Rovers, and Farrell joined Tranmere as

Peter Farrell, captain and a first-choice wing-half for the first 11 seasons after the Second World War.

player-manager in October 1957, four months after Eglington had gone in the same direction. Farrell was a strong wing-half, who captained Everton for many seasons. He managed to play 453 games for the Blues, and like Eglington appeared for both the Republic and Northern Ireland, 28 and 7 times respectively. He scored in the historic first home defeat of England in 1949. After leaving Wrexham in 1960, he managed Holyhead before returning to Ireland. He and Eglington were happy players, and very popular with the fans.

Wally Fielding.   A Londoner, he turned out 410 times for Everton from the Second World War practically to the end of the 1950s – 14 seasons in all. A small inside-forward, he was a midfield general who prompted the attack. He was spotted during the war, and his signing caused trouble because he had been on Charlton's books as an amateur before the war. He just missed winning a cap, but was a stalwart for the Blues.

Tom Fleetwood.   Joining Everton from Rochdale as a forward, he made his debut in 1910–11. He was converted to a half-back and was a tower of strength at both centre or wing-half for many years. He missed only three games in the Championship year of 1914–15. Perhaps his best years were lost to the war, both his England appearances being unofficial wartime ones. He remained with the Blues until 1922–23, completing 285 games before leaving for Oldham Athletic.

Jimmy Gabriel.   He played 300 games for Everton in the 1960s, being only 19 when he signed from Dundee in 1960. He was a very tough right-half who would never stop running. He played 40 League games in the Championship-winning season in 1962–63, and played in the exciting Cup final victory in 1966. The following season he lost his place to Howard Kendall and was transferred to Southampton. Later he played in America for Seattle Sounders. He won two Scottish caps.

Andy Gray.   Although he was not at Everton for long, his 61 appearances plus 7 as substitute were crucial to the club's modern success. A dashing centre-forward, outstanding with his head, his game was built on bravery, and his career was handicapped by the resultant injuries. He had been at Dundee United, Villa and Wolves before joining Everton in November 1983 for £250,000. He had cost Wolves £1½ million four years earlier. He scored in the FA Cup final win over Watford in 1984, and played in over half the Championship games in 1984–85. He was also valuable in Europe, scoring five goals in his three appearances, including vital ones in the Cup Winners' Cup semi-final and final. He was an inspired buy for Everton, on occasions galvanizing the team into action. He returned to Aston Villa in July 1985 for £150,000, with a job well done. Injury restricted his Scottish caps to 19.

Brian Harris.   Joining Everton as a part-timer from Port Sunlight in 1954, he was a promising outside-left who, when he established himself in the Everton side, dropped back to left-half. Eventually he became the ideal utility player, turning in a good performance wherever required. In 12 seasons at the club he made over 350 appearances, getting a Championship medal in 1962–63 and a Cup-winners' medal in 1966, when he played left-half at Wembley. The following season he left for Cardiff, and later was player-manager at Newport.

Hunter Hart.   He made his debut in January 1922 after Everton had paid Airdrie £4000 for him, and continued to play until the end of the 1920s, by which time he had registered 300 appearances, many as skipper. He was

Wally Fielding played for 14 seasons from 1945–46, when he appeared in the FA Cup. He just missed a cap, but had the honour to play for England in the unofficial international against Scotland in aid of the Bolton Disaster Fund in 1946.

usually left-half, but in the Championship year of 1927–28 was centre-half, and according to Thomas Keates' history was the 'genius of the halves'. He lost his place half-way through the 1929–30 season when Everton were relegated, and retired.

Colin Harvey. A Liverpudlian, he was especially appreciated at Goodison. He signed as a 17-year-old for Everton in 1962, made his debut in 1963 in Milan in the European Cup, and established himself in the side in 1964–65. His qualities were not obvious at first, but soon his positional sense, energy and good ball distribution became apparent. He played at inside-forward initially, winning a Cup winners' medal at inside-left 1966, but next season he was at left-half. That season Ball arrived to play inside-right, and when Kendall took over at right-half the following season, Everton's famous midfield trio was complete. None was taller than 5ft 8in. (1.73m), and all three were dynamos, whose work-rates were matched with skill. The Cup final of 1968 was lost; but the Championship of 1969–70 was safely gathered in. By now Harvey was suffering with eye trouble, and occasional injuries. His only England cap came in 1971, when he was past his best. He was transferred to Sheffield Wednesday in 1974 after nearly 400 appearances, but returned to Goodison's back room in 1976 and became first-team coach in 1983.

The men behind the team. Coach Colin Harvey shows his excitement and manager Howard Kendall looks determined to escape the embraces after the FA Cup semi-final victory against Southampton at Highbury in 1984. Trevor Steven, who had been taken off, looks worried – but his Wembley place was safe.

Adrian Heath races past Lawrie Madden of Sheffield Wednesday. His injury in 1984 meant more strikers arriving at Goodison to compete for places.

Adrian Heath.   He became Everton's most expensive signing when he was bought from Stoke in January 1982 for £700,000. He was not quite 21, only 5ft 6in. (1.68m) tall and little more than 10st (63.5kg). Perhaps manager Kendall saw him in the mould of the midfield dynamos which served Everton so well in their Championship days of 1969–70. He began playing well at forward and showed a keen awareness of goal. In 1983–84 he scored vital goals as Everton fought to two Cup finals, and he collected an FA Cup winners' medal. In the next season, the great one, he was unluckily injured against Sheffield Wednesday after 25 matches, and missed the rest of the season. He was back in 1985–86 competing hard for one of the forward positions.

Mark Higgins.   This tough Merseysider has fought back hard from an injury that almost ended his career. He joined Everton from school, signed at the age of 18 in 1976, and after appearing in spells for five seasons really established himself in 1981–82. He made the central defensive position his own, and in 1982–83 became club captain. But by the end of 1983 a pelvic problem had become apparent, and he was forced to give up the game just as the club he captained was about to perform great deeds. However, having collected the insurance, he returned it and bravely began a comeback with Manchester United in 1986.

Johnny Holt.   Bought from Bootle for the first Football League programme in 1888–89, he played for Everton through most of the 1890s, including the first match at Goodison Park. Holt was an amazing player, only 5ft 4½in. (1.64m) tall, yet he played centre-half, and was immensely powerful in the air. He played 10 times for England. He was, according to Thomas Keates' 1929 history, 'an artist in the perpetration of clever minor fouls'. He was a vital member of Everton's first Championship side in 1890–91, and extremely popular with the fans, who called him 'the Little Devil'.

John Hurst.   Born in Blackpool in 1947, he played for England schoolboys, was an Everton apprentice, signed for the club in 1964, made his debut in 1965,

John Hurst was ever-present in the 1969–70 Championship side. A schoolboy international, he became a tower of strength on the left flank for over 10 seasons.

and for eight seasons from 1967–68 was a regular, ending with nearly 400 appearances. He began playing up front in a No. 10 shirt, but eventually settled as a fine attacking left-sided midfield player. He played at Wembley in 1968, and was an ever-present in the 1969–70 Championship team.

Jimmy Husband. A Tynesider by birth, he became an apprentice with Everton and made his debut at the end of the 1964–65 season when only 17 – he was only just 18 when making his European debut. He was a popular inside-forward who was fast, skilful and unpredictable – likely to score brilliant goals but also to miss an occasional easy chance, as he did in the 1968 Cup final which Everton eventually lost. He was a regular member of the 1969–70 Championship side, making nearly 200 appearances in all, before moving to Luton in 1973.

Tommy E. Jones. Born in Liverpool in 1930, he was Everton's centre-half throughout the 1950s and a true one-club man. He played his usual dependable game over 400 times, in both the First and Second Divisions, just missing international honours and winning no major titles with Everton. But it was an exemplary club career, ended by a smashed knee cap when he had dropped into the Central League side.

Tommy G. Jones. He was the centre-half before Tommy E. Indeed a Tommy Jones appeared at centre-half for Everton every season from 1936–37 to 1961–62. Tommy G. was an intelligent man who was not content to play in the stopper style fashionable in the 1930s. He was a constructive player who always attempted to use the ball. Born in Connahs Quay, he joined Everton from Wrexham, and was soon Wales' first choice. He won a Championship medal in 1938-39, but the war came when he was at his peak. Afterwards he resumed his international career (he won 17 caps) and would have joined Roma in Italy but for a currency problem. This was nearly 10 years before John Charles went to Italy and the traffic became common. He became club captain, but fell out with the board and left League football after playing only 14 games in 1949–50.

Howard Kendall. He first became famous as the youngest player (nearly 18) to play in the Cup final (a record since lost to Paul Allen. This was for Second-Division Preston in 1964 – in March 1967 he became an Everton player for £80,000. He slotted in at right-half and was soon at Wembley again – losing for a second time in 1968. But with Ball and Harvey he formed the famous midfield trio which lifted Everton to the Championship in 1969–70. Those heights were never achieved again and in February 1974, after Clements had taken his place, he left for Birmingham City, Latchford coming the other way. Later he went to Stoke, then to Blackburn as player-manager, and in 1981, back to Everton as manager. He played four games at the end of 1981 as a non-contract player, bringing his appearances to 274. As a player, Kendall was for a long time on the brink of international honours without ever winning a cap.

Roger Kenyon. He was born in Blackpool in 1949 and signed for Everton as a 17-year-old in 1966, making his debut in 1967–68. He began as a wing-half alongside Brian Labone, but gradually took over at centre-half from the end of the Championship season, 1969–70. A car accident and a series of injuries did not help his progress, although he became club captain in the mid-1970s and was good enough to get on the England substitutes' bench in 1975. He had been substitute in the 1968 Cup final, again without getting on the field. His appearances declined from 1975–76, but he made over 300 in 12 seasons before leaving for Vancouver Whitecaps.

Andy King. An enthusiastic player, his appetite for the fray got him into all the tight situations and often led to vital goals. He was born in Luton, and was signed from his local club for £35,000 at the end of the 1975–76 season. In the following four seasons he was a regular as an aggressive midfield ball-player. But after Everton had finished 19th in 1979–80 he went to QPR for £450,000, and after one season to West Brom for another big fee. He then returned to Goodison for two seasons, but after a total of 247 appearances he was given a free transfer and went to Holland. He should have achieved more.

Brian Labone. Born in Liverpool, he was a magnificent one-club man who won many honours with club and country. He signed in July 1957 as a 17-year-old, and for two seasons deputized occasionally for Tommy Jones, but in 1959–60 he made the centre-half position his own. At 6ft 1in. (1.85m) and 13st 4lb (84.4 kg) he was a strong, defensive stopper, good in the air, but by no means a destructive player. In fact, he was a cultured footballer, who did not resort to brawn. He won a Championship medal in 1962–63, led his team to Cup final victory at Wembley in 1966, and won another Championship medal in 1969–70. He made three appearances for England in 1963, but was not picked again until after the 1966 World Cup success. However, he was first choice from 1968 and played in the World Cup finals in Mexico in 1970. Altogether he won 26 caps. He appeared for Everton in 15 seasons. An Achilles tendon injury ended his career when he had made 533 appearances.

Rising high above the Welsh defence and his Everton team-mate Alan Ball, Brian Labone was a model centre-half for both club and country.

£350,000 signing Bob Latchford displays his skills to Billy Bingham, the 1960s winger who returned to manage the club, and to his new chairman, John Moores.

Bob Latchford.   He joined Everton in February 1974 with a big reputation as a goalscorer. The fee, which included Howard Kendall, was estimated at £350,000. He was an old-fashioned type of centre-forward, good with his head. Apparently slow and clumsy on the ground, he nevertheless managed to score regularly and often, and in 1976 he led the First-Division list with 30 goals, claiming the £10,000 which the *Daily Express* had offered to anyone reaching this mark. In 1977 he won the first of 12 England caps. After 289 appearances and 138 goals he left in July 1981 for Swansea City, and later was on Coventry's and Lincoln's books.

Tommy Lawton.   He was the natural successor to Dixie Dean. It is remarkable that England's two greatest centre-forwards followed each other at Everton. Lawton was born in Bolton and made his League debut for Burnley just four days after his 17th birthday. Everton paid £6500 for him in March 1937, and for the remainder of the season he either replaced Dean or played alongside him. For the last two seasons before the war, however, he was the centre-forward, topping the First-Division scorers' lists and winning a Championship medal. He played eight times for England before the war, and scored 70 goals for Everton in 95 games. Amazingly, he was still a teenager when the war started, and of course his career was seriously affected. Afterwards he joined Chelsea, then Third-Division Notts County (for the then-record fee of £20,000), then Brentford, then back to the top flight with Arsenal. He played for England 23 times and scored 22 goals. In wartime internationals he averaged more than a goal a game. He was the complete centre-forward.

Tommy Lawton, the teenage prodigy who replaced Dixie Dean not only as Everton's centre-forward but also as the fans' new hero.

Gary Lineker.   A goalscorer of a different kind from Evertonians Lawton, Dean and Latchford, he arrived at Goodison in time for the 1985–86 season, fighting for a place in a team that had just won the Championship and reached two Cup finals. Born in Leicester, City had been his only club. In just over 200 games for them he had scored more than 100 goals. A clever, sharp striker (as opposed to an out-and-out centre-forward), his assets are quickness to see a chance and the control to convert it. He made his England debut in May 1984 as a substitute, and went on the following summer tour. In 1985–86, as Everton soared to the top of the League again, Lineker developed an understanding with Sharp and began to score prolifically, notching up 40 goals by the end of the season.

Mick Lyons.   Throughout the 1970s he played his heart out for Everton. Born in Liverpool, he signed in 1969 while still 17. Most of his appearances up to 1975–76 were as a forward, but in that season he was ever-present in midfield, and was soon club captain. Eventually he became centre-back. In February 1982 he lost this place to Billy Wright. He decided to move on, and after more than 450 games for the Blues he was transferred to Sheffield Wednesday for £100,000, captaining them to the First Division as an ever-present in 1983–84.

Harry Makepeace.   He was born in Middlesbrough but played soccer for Everton and England and cricket for Lancashire and England. He joined Everton as an employee, was given a trial in the reserves, with a little added to his wages, and did so well that he relinquished his job and became a footballer. He was a fine half-back who shone in the Cup final win in 1906. After several near-misses he won a Championship medal in his last season, 1914–15, when he completed 336 appearances. His four soccer matches for England were from 1906 to 1912. His Test matches were in 1920–21, when in his 40th year – at Melbourne against Australia he became the oldest player to score a maiden Test century. By then he was also the Everton coach.

Joe Mercer.   Born at Ellesmere Port in 1914, he signed for Everton in 1932. He was a regular in 1935–36 and missed only one game in the Championship win in 1938–39. By then he had established a reputation as a clever constructive left-half, and in that season he made his five appearances for England. As with Lawton, the war came at the worst time for his career. Afterwards, he could not settle, and Arsenal signed him in December 1946 for £7000 on a short-term basis. But, as captain of Arsenal, he had a brilliant second career with two Championship medals and a victory at Wembley in the Cup final. His bandy legs were famous in football, and it was a sad fracture of one which finally ended his playing career. Later he was successful as a manager at Aston Villa and Manchester City and as a caretaker for England. During his Arsenal days he trained at Anfield, and he continues to live locally, at Hoylake.

John Morrissey.   He was born in Liverpool and signed for the Reds in 1957. A well-built outside-left, he was transferred to the Blues in 1962. It took a while for him to establish a regular place, and he missed the 1966 Cup final, although he played at Wembley in 1968. He missed only one game in the 1969–70 Championship success. Two years later he moved to Oldham Athletic. He played over 300 games for Everton, scoring 50 goals.

Derek Mountfield.   Born in Liverpool in 1962, he signed for Tranmere when he was 18. Eighteen months later he joined Everton for £30,000. He got an early chance to establish a central defensive place in 1983–84, bringing back an FA Cup winners' medal from Wembley. He is a mobile defensive player who prefers to play out of trouble, and in 1984–85 he not only helped out the midfield but the strikers too, with 14 goals. They helped him add a Championship and a European Cup Winners' Cup medal to his collection.

Keith Newton.   A full-back of class, he did not do himself justice at Everton, not seeing eye-to-eye with Harry Catterick. He arrived in 1969 after over 300 games for Blackburn Rovers. He had already appeared in 19 internationals for England as an attacking full-back, and he and his new Everton colleague,

Top *Harold Makepeace in 1913–14. Only two men, apart from him, have played four or more internationals and four or more Test matches.*

Above *Although his career was disrupted by the war, Joe Mercer was a regular for Everton before it, and later made a new career for himself at Arsenal.*

Following pages *Gary Lineker came from Leicester in 1985–86 to make Everton's strike force even stronger. He quickly began scoring heavily. Here he is playing against Arsenal.*

Above *Captain Kevin Ratcliffe with the Canon League First-Division trophy.*

Opposite top *Joe Royle was Everton's youngest player when he made his debut on 15 January 1966, three months short of his 17th birthday. He was ever-present in the 1969–70 Championship season. A young Ray Clemence has gathered the ball at his feet.*

Opposite middle *Ted Sagar played for Everton in 1929–30, before the most famous team in the world, Arsenal, had won a single major trophy, and despite losing eight years to the war, played his 495th senior match for Everton in 1952–53.*

Opposite below *Graeme Sharp scored 30 goals in the 1984–85 season, and struck up an attacking partnership with Gary Lineker in 1985–86 which promised goals for Everton for many years.*

Right *Peter Reid, the footballers' own Player of the Year in 1985, whose form in an Indian summer won him an England cap.*

Tommy Wright, shared the right-back spot in England's 1970 World Cup games in Mexico. On his return, however, he lost his place in both the Everton and England teams, and left for Burnley in 1972. He played only 58 games for Everton, a disappointment.

Jimmy O'Neill. Born in Dublin in 1931, he joined Everton in 1949. He made his debut as a goalkeeper in 1950, but could not keep his place as the team slid to relegation. He got back next season in the Second Division, and was first choice until Everton forced their way back to the First Division. He won 17 caps for the Republic of Ireland while at Goodison. From the 1956 to 1957 season Albert Dunlop was preferred, and in 1960 O'Neill went to Stoke for £5000.

Kevin Ratcliffe. He signed for Everton as soon as he was 18, in November 1978. He was born in Mankot, Wales, and was a schoolboy international. He made his debut at the end of the 1979–80 season, and over the next three seasons gradually played his way into the first team, mostly at left-back. Not liking his position, he asked for a transfer. Luckily he forced his way into a central defensive spot, first with Mark Higgins, then with Derek Mountfield, and hasn't looked back. His speed enables him to cover well and he is good with his head. In December 1983 he was made captain, and soon was receiving the FA Cup at Wembley. In 1984–85 it was the Championship and the European Cup Winners' Cup. There were two other finals in those seasons, and there was no let-up in 1985–86, as Everton and the young captain forced their way to the top of the First Division again. He was first capped by Wales in 1980, and has been an automatic choice since.

Peter Reid. Having overcome a catalogue of injuries with Bolton Wanderers, he has built a second and more illustrious career with Everton. He was born at Huyton in 1956, signed for Bolton when 18 and made over 250 appearances for them in eight years. He was a dynamo of a right-half, hard-tackling but constructive, a ball-winner and user. He attracted the big clubs, including Everton, for whom Gordon Lee offered £600,000 for him. But he ran into a series of serious leg injuries, ranging from a broken knee-cap in 1978 to a broken leg in 1981. Eventually Howard Kendall bought him for £60,000 in

December 1982. It was soon to prove a bargain, as the broken-down workhorse made over 50 appearances in 1983–84 and won himself a Cup winners' medal. The following season he repeated the treatment, winning a Championship medal, a European Cup Winners' Cup medal, the PFA 'Player of the Year' accolade and a first England cap. Injury in 1985–86 halted him for a while, but as he approached 30 the football gods were at last being kind to him.

Joe Royle. Liverpool-born, he signed for Everton as soon as he could, making his debut towards the end of the 1965–66 season, before his 17th birthday. He became a regular in 1967–68, and from 11 May 1968 began a run of 128 consecutive games, which ended in January 1971. At 6ft (1.83m) tall and weighing 13st 2lb (83.5kg) he was a natural, strong centre-forward, fast and commanding in the air. He was on the losing side at Wembley in 1968, but was an ever-present in the Championship side of 1969–70, scoring 23 of Everton's 72 goals. He just missed selection for the Mexico World Cup in 1970, but later won six England caps, most of these coming after he had left Everton in December 1974. In 273 appearances he had scored 119 goals. He played for Manchester City, Bristol City and Norwich City before injury forced his retirement in 1982 and he took up managership.

Ted Sagar. He was a professional with Everton for more than 24 years – a record for a one-club man. Not surprisingly, his 463 League games are a club record. He was born in Moorend in 1910 and was signed by Everton after Hull City had given him a trial. He made his debut in goal on 18 January 1930, and kept a clean sheet against Derby County. He did not play in 1930–31, missing the club's season in the Second Division, but he missed only one match the following year, when Everton took the Championship. He was first choice until the Second World War, keeping a clean sheet at Wembley in 1933 to win a Cup winners' medal, and adding a second Championship medal in 1938–39. He won four caps in the 1935–36 season. After the war, he was back as good as ever. From 1949–50 he began sharing the jersey with his younger challengers. In his last two seasons, Everton were in the Second Division, and he made his last 11 appearances in the Division he had avoided over 20 years earlier. His last match was on 15 November 1952 at Plymouth.

Billy Scott. This Belfast-born goalkeeper joined Everton from Linfield in 1904. He was already a Northern Ireland international and he eventually won 25 caps, a large number in those days. He played in two Cup finals, on the winning side in 1906, when he played superbly. He made 289 appearances for Everton before departing for Leeds City in 1912. His younger brother was the more famous Elisha, whom Billy recommended to Liverpool, and who succeeded him in the Irish goal, winning 31 caps up to 1936.

Graeme Sharp. He was only 19 when Everton bought him for £120,000 from Dumbarton at the end of the 1979–80 season. Midway through the 1981–82 season he established a regular place in attack. He is a fast and clever striker, equally at home as the leader of the attack or playing alongside a conventional leader like Andy Gray. He is a good all-round footballer with a quick eye for a chance, which sometimes leads to unexpected goals. With the arrival of Andy Gray in 1983–84, there was great competition for the Everton striking roles, and Sharp's form, if anything, became sharper. He scored at Wembley in the 1984 Cup final, was a vital member of the 1984–85 Championship side (top-scorer with 21), and won a European Cup Winners' Cup medal. His progress continued in 1985–86, when he established a powerful scoring partnership with newcomer Gary Lineker. He made his debut for Scotland in May 1985.

Jack Sharp. He played in the 19th century, making his debut in 1899, and was a first choice until 1910. He was a right-winger, born in Hereford and having a short stay at Villa before arriving at Goodison. A sprinter, accurate with his centres and possessing a hard shot, he set up the winning goal in the 1906 Cup final. He made two appearances for England in 1903 and 1905. Like his team-mate, Harry Makepeace, he played cricket for Lancashire, and, again like him, was a double international, playing three Tests against Australia in 1909. Extraordinarily, again like Makepeace, he made a century. He was a tremendous all-round sportsman, making 300 League and 42 Cup appearances for Everton, and playing 518 times for Lancashire over 26 seasons. His brother Bert was also an Evertonian, and Jack and his son were both directors of the club.

Kevin Sheedy. Born in Builth Wells in 1959, he joined Hereford United in 1976 and two years later was signed by Bob Paisley for Liverpool. Four years and only three League appearances later, he became the first player for many years to move from Liverpool to Everton; the fee was £100,000. Sheedy immediately got first-team football and has been a regular ever since. He is an excellent left-sided midfield player, can fill the role of an orthodox winger and is a regular goalscorer, being particularly good at free-kicks. He has had one or two injuries, and missed the Cup final in 1985. He has played for the Republic of Ireland since 1983–84.

Neville Southall. He is the most improved goalkeeper in the League, and arguably the best. Born in Llandudno in 1958 he was originally a centre-back who was turned down by professional clubs before he moved into goal, when Bury spotted him and bought him for £6000 from Cheshire League side Winsford in 1980. After 44 appearances in his only season there, Howard Kendall paid £150,000 for him in July 1981. He took over from Jim Arnold in the Everton goal around Christmas time, but after Liverpool had won 5–0 at Goodison on 6 November 1982, he was dropped, and in January 1983 was loaned to Port Vale, making nine appearances in the Third Division. He returned for the last three games of the season. He did not get into the first team until the eighth game of 1983–84, but from then he was ever-present for the rest of the season and the next, through the two winning and two losing Cup finals and the Championship success. Brilliant reflexes allow him to make astonishing point-blank saves. He is now an automatic choice for Wales, having made his debut in 1982, and in 1985 he was the Football Writers' Association 'Footballer of the Year'.

Trevor Steven. Born in Berwick, he signed for Burnley in 1981 when he was 18 years old. Two years later Howard Kendall paid £300,000 for him and he went straight into the first team, where he has remained, except for a spell in 1983–84 when Alan Irvine wore the No. 7 shirt. Steven is a right-sided midfielder with speed and brilliant dribbling skills who, when Everton are attacking, plays like the outside-rights of old. He won a Cup winners' medal in 1984, although missing the Milk Cup finals, and missed only two games in the triumphant 1984–85 Championship season, scoring in both the semi-final and final of the European Cup Winners' Cup. He made his England debut in February 1985.

Gary Stevens. He joined Everton as an apprentice and signed in April 1981 when he was 18. He made his debut at right-back the following season, and took over finally from Brian Borrows early in the 1982–83 season. He is very fast, and a fine attacking full-back, which was ideal for Everton as they began their all-conquering run in 1983–84. He played on all the big occasions in that and the following season, winning FA Cup, European Cup Winners' Cup and Championship medals. In 1985 he made his England debut against Italy on the summer tour to America.

Alex Stevenson.   One of those players whose career was disrupted by the Second World War, he was born in Dublin in 1912 and made a big reputation as a brilliant ball-playing inside-left with Glasgow Rangers. He was only 5ft 3in. (1.60m) tall, but was well-built and balanced enough to withstand the fiercest tackling. He was signed by Everton in 1934, just after the Championship and Cup wins, and joined Dean in a star-studded forward line. He was a regular till the war, winning a Championship medal in the last pre-war season. He returned for three seasons afterwards, finally retiring in 1949 with 271 appearances. His left-wing partnership with Jackie Coulter was famous for both Everton and Ireland, for whom Stevenson made 17 appearances for Northern Ireland and seven for the Republic.

Alex Stevenson, born in Dublin, made his name with Glasgow Rangers, joining Everton in 1934. He stayed till 1949, and was a Republic of Ireland international for 17 years.

Jack Taylor.   He played in three FA Cup finals for Everton. He was 'one of the most loyal, energetic and gifted players the Club ever engaged', to quote the 1929 historian Keates, and 'played anywhere readily, and played well everywhere'. From 1896 to 1910, he played 456 times for Everton. In the 1897 Cup final he was on the wing, in 1906 and 1907 at centre-half – as captain he collected the Cup on the first occasion. His career came to an end in the semi-final replay in 1910 against Barnsley when the ball struck him in the larynx and injured him severely.

Derek Temple.   Liverpool-born, he signed for Everton in 1956 from the juniors, making his debut in 1956–57. A stocky, fast striker, for seven seasons he was in and out of the team in all the forward positions, making only five appearances in the Championship year of 1962–63. But next season he at last got an extended run, taking over from Morrissey at outside-left and missing only one League game. In May 1965 he played for England for the only time. His biggest moment came in the 1966 Cup final, when he scored the dramatic winner in the 3-2 victory over Sheffield Wednesday. In 1967 he left Goodison for Preston after 273 appearances.

Jock Thomson.   A Scot who joined Everton from Dundee in 1930 and played through to the war, his first full season was in the Second Division, which the Blues won, and the second brought him a Championship medal and his only Scottish cap. He was a strong, forceful player at left-half, and he added to his Championship medal with a Cup winners' medal the following year. The arrival of Joe Mercer in 1935–36 was the first threat to his position, and he played little in the next two seasons, but he returned with 26 League appearances in his second Championship season of 1938–39. He retired, and after the war managed Manchester City for a while.

Alec Troup, Scottish international winger, looks cold at White Hart Lane in January 1926.

Alec Troup.   A star of the 1920s, he was a tiny 5ft 5in. (1.65m) Scottish left-winger, who joined Everton from Dundee in January 1923. He was a brilliant dribbler and could cross with such accuracy that the ball seemed to hang, waiting for Dean to head it in. He had to play with a weak collarbone strapped up. He won only five Scottish caps – his career coincided with the immortal Wee Blue Devil, Alan Morton. He played 259 times for Everton, and was ever-present in the Championship year of 1928 (he was second in the goal-scoring list with 10). This was the season Dean scored his record 60 goals. It may not be Troup's least claim to fame that in the celebration speeches at the North-

Preceding pages *Action in the 1968 Cup final against West Bromwich Albion, which Albion won 1–0. The goalscorer, Jeff Astle, leaps high for a cross, but Gordon West has beaten him to the ball to punch clear.*

Roy Vernon, club captain during the championship season of 1962-63.

Ray Wilson, only 153 appearances for the Blues, but the perfect full-back.

Western Hotel dinner on the night of his record, Dean emphasized the credit due to Alec.

Pat van den Hauwe.   He was born in Belgium on 16 December 1960 and was brought to London when a boy. He signed for Birmingham City in 1978, and had made 140 appearances for them when Howard Kendall paid £100,000 for him early in the 1984–85 season, and he immediately replaced John Bailey at left-back. A hard tackler, he is very strong defensively, and in 1985–86 he began to show a more adventurous side to his game with left-wing raids. He won a Championship medal in his first season and played in the later rounds in the European Cup Winners' Cup. He is ineligible for Belgium, having declined to do National Service, and chose to represent Wales, by whom he was first picked in April 1985.

Roy Vernon.   A brilliant inside-left, he preferred to join Blackburn Rovers rather than Everton when he signed professional forms in 1955. After 131 League games, 49 goals and nine Welsh caps, he was brought to Goodison for £27,000 plus Eddie Thomas in February 1960. He went straight into the first team and maintained the all-round form he had shown since a teenager. He became club captain, and missed only one League game in the Championship season in 1962–63. In March 1965 he moved on to Stoke for £40,000 having played 199 times and scored an impressive 110 goals. He continued playing until 1970, and won 32 caps.

Gordon West.   Despite being born in Barnsley he first signed for Blackpool, in 1961. Less than a year later Harry Catterick paid a record fee for a goalkeeper of £27,000 to bring him to Goodison. West was a strong, bouncy goalie, who in his first full season with the Blues won a Championship medal. For the next three seasons Andy Rankin sometimes claimed his place, but he was in goal when the FA Cup was won in 1966, and, less happily, when it was lost in 1968. In 1969 he made three appearances for England as understudy for Gordon Banks, but surprised the football world by declining to join the World Cup squad in Mexico in 1970 – Stepney was picked instead. He was ever-present in 1969–70 to win his second Championship medal, but Andy Rankin was preferred next season, and West played in only the first of the European Cup games. He fought back and was ever-present again in 1971–72 but next year Everton again broke the goalkeeper's transfer record when buying David Lawson, and West retired with 399 appearances. He came back for Tranmere and played 17 League games from seasons 1976–77 to 1978–79.

Ray Wilson.   He made only 153 appearances for Everton in his five seasons, but he was one of the Everton men who helped win the World Cup in 1966. He made his name with Huddersfield, moving to Everton in July 1964 for £40,000. He was a perfect full-back, strong in the tackle, fast, good positionally and always ready to attack. He won a Cup winners' medal in 1966 and was at Wembley again in 1968. A knee injury in training for the following season, however, virtually ended his career. He won 63 caps for England.

Tommy Wright.   Another World Cup full-back, when he joined the juniors from school he was actually an inside-forward, and he gradually moved back through the team. He made his debut late in 1964, and was a regular the following season, partnering Ray Wilson and winning a Cup winners' medal. He was not so lucky at Wembley in 1968, but was ever-present when the Championship was won in 1969–70. Wright was a constructive full-back who joined team-mate Wilson in the England team in 1968, and his eventual 11

caps included the 1970 World Cup finals in Mexico. He had made 371 appearances for Everton when he retired in 1973.

Alex (Sandy) Young.   A Scotsman who joined Everton from Falkirk in 1901, he made 314 appearances up to the 1910–11 season, and although Everton could do no better than three times runners-up in the League, Young had his big moment in 1906. An international centre-forward (he won two caps), he scored the only goal which brought the Cup to Goodison for the first time. The noise which greeted the goal and the reception of the team back at Liverpool were both described as shattering.

Alex Young.   Another famous Scottish centre-forward who joined Everton from Hearts in 1960 for about £40,000, he was an instinctive footballer, who occasionally produced touches of such stunning skill that he became a cult figure, with his blond hair leading to the sobriquet 'The Golden Vision'. In his second full season, 1962–63, Everton won the Championship, with Young an ever-present. He had delicate feet, and was prone to minor injuries, and in the following seasons missed 15 or 20 games, but he was always ready for the big occasion, such as the 1966 Cup final, in which he won a winners' medal. In January that year, Young had been left out for Joe Royle to make his debut, and Harry Catterick had been assaulted by Young fans. Young had drifted out of the team by the time of the 1968 final, and went off to manage Glentoran, soon returning for a season at Stockport. He won eight Scottish caps and played 271 games for Everton. A very funny television play about a group of Everton fans was called 'The Golden Vision' after Young, the idol of the terraces.

Tommy Wright, here seen in action against Brazil in the World Cup Finals in Mexico, was a one-club man who made 371 appearances for Everton between 1964 and 1973, as well as earning 11 England caps.

Following pages *Neville Southall makes a sure catch as David Armstrong of Southampton waits for a mistake, which practically never comes where Southall is concerned.*

HAFNIA
HAFNIA
EFC
AIR FLORIDA
DANEPAK
CINZANO

KODACOLOR FILM

Famous Matches

Preceding pages *Gordon West in action in the 1966 FA Cup final. Sheffield Wednesday took a two-goal lead before Everton fought back.*

This chapter includes descriptions of 10 of the best or most significant matches in Everton's history.

FA Cup final, 1906

Everton 1   Newcastle United 0

In the 1890s Everton had twice reached the final of the FA Cup, and on 21 April 1906 were at the Crystal Palace to play Newcastle United, the great Cup-fighting side of the day (they appeared in five finals in seven years).

Everton had beaten Liverpool in the semi-final, when Merseyside invaded Villa Park. Late in the game Walter Abbott and Harold Hardman had scored for a 2–0 victory. Liverpool became Champions and Everton were to bring the Cup back to the city at last.

Both sides prepared for the final by fielding weak teams in the League and were consequently fined. Large crowds went down to the match – 'Crystal Palace besieged' said *The Liverpool Football Echo* headline. The attendance was given as 75,609. The match started at 3.30 p.m., and the same paper noted the cinematograph man grinding away the film, and confessed to palpitations all round at the sight of Colin Veitch, Newcastle's famous international forward.

After four minutes the match was stopped while the referee spoke to all the players as play became heated. The Blues had done all the attacking. Newcastle had a polished half-back line, including the Scot, Peter McWilliam, but they were being overrun, although play became scrappy and half-chances were missed. The *Football Echo's* minute-by-minute account has this sequence: '3.43 – Poor play in midfield. 3.44 – The same. 3.45 – Worse.

Everton pressed again after a goalless first half and after 10 minutes Sandy

The team which won the FA Cup in 1905–06. The actual Cup on display is the second, the first having been stolen from a shop in Birmingham while held by Aston Villa. This Cup was presented to Lord Kinnaird, who appeared in nine Cup finals, in 1910, after which the present Cup was awarded. Team, left to right, back: Jack Elliott (trainer); Harry Makepeace; Walter Balmer; Jack Taylor (captain); Billy Scott; Jack Crelley; Walter Abbott. Front: Jack Sharp; H. Bolton; Alex 'Sandy' Young; Jimmy Settle; Harold Hardman. Makepeace and Sharp were both 'double' internationals at football and cricket.

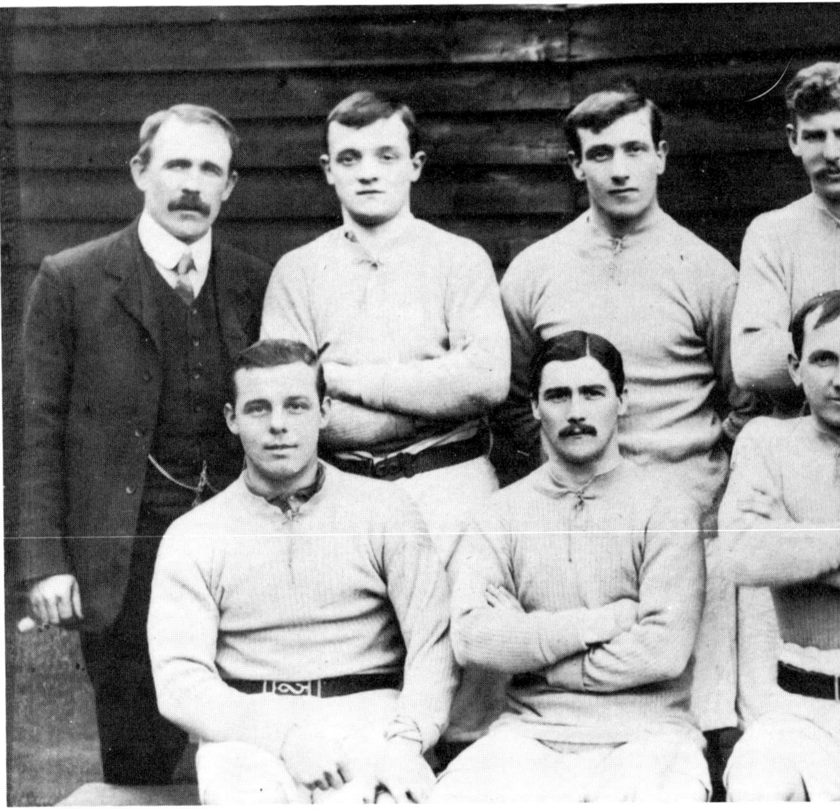

Young put the ball in the net, but was ruled offside. Then Newcastle began to counter and Billy Scott was forced to make a good save. Jimmy Settle almost scored in the corner for the Blues, and Newcastle remained on the defensive.

Finally, with less than a quarter of an hour left, Everton scored. Jack Sharp set it up, beating two players before centring for Young to turn home. 'Fireworks and miniature earthquakes in galore... the big glasshouse shakes at its foundations', said the *Echo* reporter. The match was a few days after the famous San Francisco earthquake.

Everton held on and took the Cup, but the celebrations were different in those days. First the players were cheered to their hotel. After dinner and speeches they went by motor bus to the Alhambra music hall where they got a big ovation. On Sunday they visited Hampton Court (can one see modern winners visiting Hampton Court next day?), then had dinner with the Newcastle players. On Monday they went to Sheffield and lost their last League match, to Wednesday. Only after that was there a special train, decorated with flags, to take them back to Central Station. Met by the Lord Mayor, the team then proceeded on a four-in-hand to Goodison, with Jack Taylor, the captain, showing the Cup to the crowds on the route. Then more speeches, and refreshments in what was described as 'the most remarkable popular demonstration that has ever taken place within the city boundaries'.

The following year the team returned to the Palace, but lost 2–1 to a last-minute goal from Sheffield Wednesday.

Teams: *Everton:* Scott; Balmer (W.), Crelley, Makepeace, Taylor, Abbott, Sharp, Bolton, Young, Settle, H.P. Hardman.
Newcastle United: Lawrence; McCombie, Carr, Gardner, Aitken, McWilliam, Rutherford, Howie, Veitch, Orr, Gosnell.

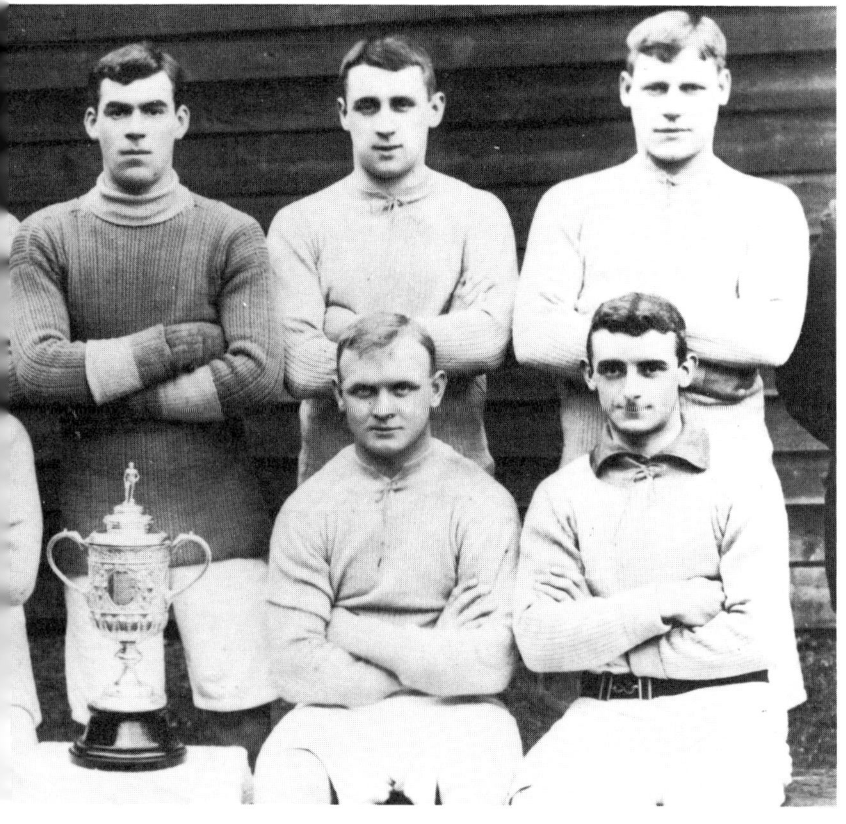

FA Cup final, 1933

Everton 3   Manchester City 0

In 1933 Everton made their first appearance at Wembley. It was the first final in which the players were numbered. The numbering began at the top of the programme with the Everton goalkeeper and continued row by row to the Manchester City goalkeeper. Thus Everton were 1–11 in today's fashion, while Manchester City were 12–22 with the outside-left being 12 and the goalie 22. Because both teams' colours were blue, both changed – Everton played in white and City in red.

Everton had to make a tricky choice between Albert Geldard, who had made his debut that season, and the old-stager Ted Critchley, the regular winger for years who had stepped in for the quarter- and semi-finals, and who had forced a late winner in the semis. Geldard, having returned from injury after the semi-final, kept his place.

City's centre-forward, Fred Tilson, was unavailable, but they had a strong side, including international centre-half and skipper Sam Cowan, future Scottish international Matt Busby, and Jimmy McMullan, captain of the 1928 Scottish Wembley Wizards, now playing his last game. Everton's Jimmy Dunn was also a Wembley Wizard, while Dixie Dean had been in the England side that was beaten that day. Alec Herd was centre-forward for City. His son, David, later played for Arsenal and Manchester United. Both won Cup winners' medals.

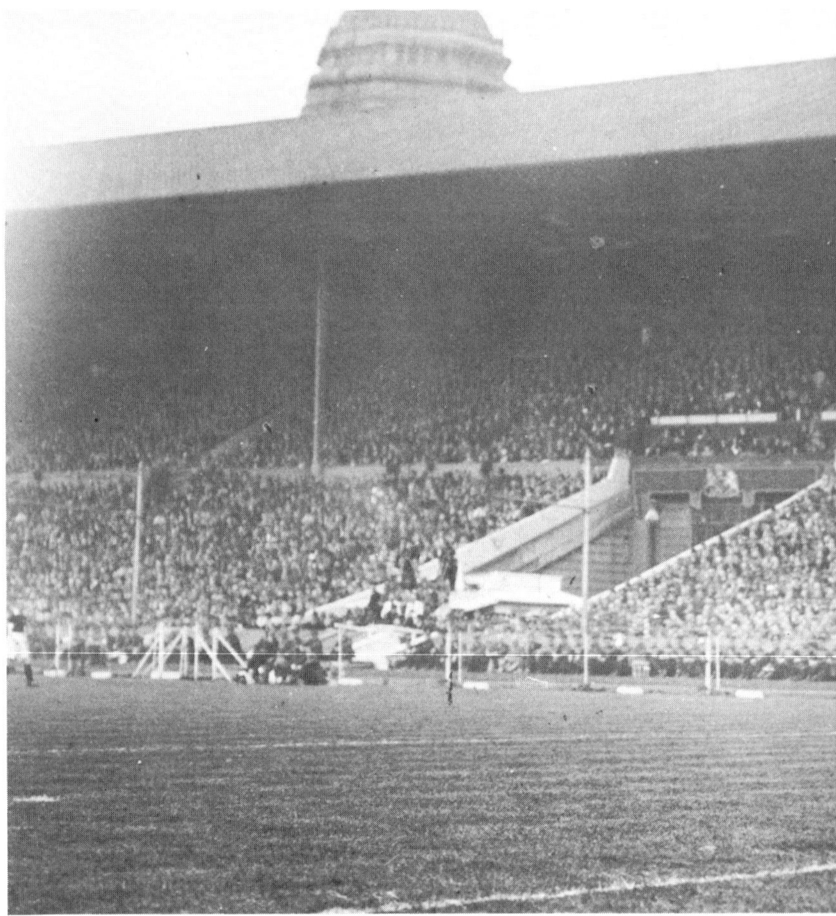

The opening goal in the 1933 Cup final. A challenge by Dean (beside goalkeeper – numbered 22) forced Langford to drop the ball and Jimmy Stein dashed in to score.

Forty special trains left Lancashire for Wembley with around 30,000 fans aboard. The official attendance was 95,920, with the Duke of York, soon to be King George VI, the guest of honour. He was accompanied by the present Queen Mother who was to hand the Cup to Dean.

City attacked from the kick-off but faded badly. It was said that they arrived at Wembley too early for the match and that the long wait in the dressing room had caused an outbreak of nerves. Everton gradually got on top and four minutes from half-time left-winger Jimmy Stein scored after Dean, with a strong challenge, had forced the goalkeeper to drop a cross from Cliff Britton.

Seven minutes after the interval goalkeeper Langford was in trouble again with another Britton cross, and this time Dean forced the ball home himself. City could not trouble the calm Everton defence, which exuded confidence from Ted Sagar in goal and the classy veteran Warney Cresswell. City, on the other hand, were never happy against the rampaging Dean, who was captain, and it was no surprise when 10 minutes from the end Geldard centred and Jimmy Dunn scored a third. Victory by three goals has been equalled but not beaten in any FA Cup final at Wembley. The victorious team were greeted back at Liverpool by a coach-and-four, echoing the reception of the 1906 Cup winners. City were to win the Cup the following year.

Teams: *Everton:* Sagar; Cook, Cresswell, Britton, White, Thomson, Geldard, Dunn, Dean, Johnson, Stein.
Manchester City: Langford; Cann, Dale, Busby, Cowan, Bray, Toseland, Marshall, Herd, McMullan, Brook.

Jimmy Stein, who opened the scoring in the 1933 Cup final.

FA Cup fourth round, 1935

Everton 6   Sunderland 4

Some football matches live in the memory for their own sakes – the context and the significance of the result become blurred, and the match itself becomes the legend.

Such was an FA Cup fourth-round replay at Goodison in January 1935. The sides had drawn 1–1 at Roker Park, and 59,213 crowded in to see the continuation. They weren't to see any tame draw!

The sides were among the strongest in the land. Sunderland were to finish runners-up in the Championship, Everton eighth. The Blues began well; left-winger Jackie Coulter, a brilliant goal-scoring Irishman, scored the first two goals on the quarter- and half-hour marks, and Everton, having most of the game territorially, seemed to be on their way. But Sunderland, with the young Raich Carter at inside-forward, fought back and four minutes before the interval his wing partner Davis reduced the arrears.

It was a goal from Alex Stevenson early in the second half that really set the match alight. Two down again, Sunderland went over to all-out attack, while Everton, with their experienced defence, settled down to keep them out. But a backpass did not reach Sagar – Sunderland's Connor got there first and it was 3–2. Then, when the Blues looked to have won, centre-forward Gurney scored a brilliant last-minute goal and it was extra-time.

Everton were now forced to attack again, and within two minutes Jackie Coulter scored his third, but Connor equalized that one, and at 4–4 the crowd could hardly take any more. Then Albert Geldard, one of the fastest wingers the game has seen, raced clear of the Sunderland defence and put Everton back in front again. And with a minute left he scored again to complete a 6–4 victory which left everybody exhausted.

Ten goals, and not one for the great Dean. In fact, eight goals were shared by the four wingers – this must approach some sort of record.

Sadly Everton went out in the sixth round – having beaten Derby at home, they lost 2–1 to Bolton Wanderers at Goodison. It was Sunderland who went on to bigger things – the Championship in the following season and the Cup in the one after that.

Teams: *Everton:* Sagar; Cook, Jones, Britton, Gee, Thomson, Geldard, Cunliffe, Dean, Stevenson, Coulter.
Sunderland: Thorpe; Murray, Hall, Thompson, Johnston, Hastings, Davis, Carter, Curney, Gallacher, Connor.

FA Cup final, 1966

Everton 3   Sheffield Wednesday 2

The 1966 Cup final is remembered as the one Sheffield Wednesday lost, the one with the unlikeliest two-goal hero, the one with the most appalling defensive blunder, or the one with the most thrilling winner. It all depends on which side it is viewed from. All four statements have a degree of truth.

Everton provided a surprise with one of those selection decisions which attract the pre-match headlines. Mike Trebilcock, a 21-year-old £20,000 signing from Plymouth Argyle in mid-season, had subsequently played eight games for the Blues, most of them at inside-forward in Alex Young's place. For the final, Harry Catterick picked him at the expense not of Young, but of centre-forward Fred Pickering, an England choice 18 months earlier, and who had missed only five games all season and was leading scorer. Trebilcock's name was not even on the programme. To the average fan he was unknown.

Wednesday were underdogs but they played excellent football. After only four minutes they were ahead when Jim McCalliog's shot took a deflection off Ray Wilson. It was the first Cup goal scored against Everton that season in eight games – for 664 minutes Gordon West had kept a clean sheet.

Wednesday kept their lead up to half-time – deservedly, although there was a powerful case for a penalty when a dive by Wednesday's England goalkeeper, Ron Springett, brought down Alex Young.

After the interval Young was foiled by a brilliant save from Springett, and then Wednesday struck again. John Fantham dribbled right through and when his shot rebounded from West's chest, David Ford was on hand to fire the ball home. There were 33 minutes to go and Everton's chances appeared to be minimal.

Everything changed the next minute, however, and it was Trebilcock, the controversial choice, who began the fight-back. Harris and Temple set up a chance and his right-foot half-volley flew into the net. Five minutes later Wednesday's reserve centre-half, Sam Ellis, standing in for the injured Vic Mobley, failed to head clear decisively enough and sharp-shooting Trebilcock flashed another right-footer past Springett. Two Everton fans invaded the pitch at this point, and threw Trebilcock to the ground in their enthusiasm. This was new behaviour for Wembley and the police stamped on it sharply.

Wednesday were now hanging on, and it appeared that their first-half speed and industry were now telling on their strength. In the 80th minute West punted upfield and Gerry Young, the Wednesday left-half, messed up a simple trap just inside his own half. As the ball slid from his boot, Derek Temple flashed past at speed, picked up the loose ball and advanced on Springett, who had time to spit on his hands as he came out to narrow the angle. As the two players closed on each other, it was like a Wild West shoot-out. Temple shot at exactly the right time and perfectly. Springett had no chance. It was a picture goal and it decided one of the best of Cup finals.

Teams: *Everton:* West; Wright, Wilson, Gabriel, Labone, Harris, Scott, Trebilcock, Young (A.), Harvey, Temple.
Sheffield Wednesday: Springett; Smith, Megson, Eustace, Ellis, Young (G.), Pugh, Fantham, McCalliog, Ford, Quinn.

Following pages *Alex Young is brought down by Ron Springett with Wednesday one up – appeals for a penalty were ignored.*

EVERTON 0 SHEFFIELD WED. 1

Milk Cup fifth round, 1984

Oxford United 1   Everton 1

Occasionally in the history of a football club, one match can be identified as having a significance much greater than is apparent at the time, with ripples which spread far from the impact it makes on the records of the competition and season which contain it.

One such was a Milk Cup fifth-round match on 18 January 1984. The contestants could hardly have been more different. Everton, founder members of the Football League, had registered more seasons, matches, wins and goals in the First Division of that league than any other club in the country. Oxford United had changed their name from Headington United only 24 years earlier, and had been in the League for only 22 years. They were a Third-Division side but were on the way up – two seasons later they had reached the First Division. While Everton were not exactly on the way down, they were having a very poor season. They had just dropped to 18th in the League, their lowest for four years, and there was constant newspaper speculation about the future of the manager, Howard Kendall.

A crowd of 14,333 watched the game at the Manor Ground, but millions more watched the progress of Everton and the exciting Oxford that Wednesday night on television. Southall was always the busier keeper but Oxford had to wait until the second half to score. A Brock free-kick to the far post was headed back by Briggs, and McDonald, the free-scoring full-back Oxford had obtained from Manchester City, put them ahead. Everton brought Kevin Richardson on for Johnson, but Oxford might well have scored again and a ragged Everton were playing without much spirit. They looked as if they had accepted defeat.

Then, with less than 10 minutes to go, Oxford's Under-21 England international, Kevin Brock, attempted an ambitious pass back to his goalkeeper, Steve Hardwick, and was horrified to see Adrian Heath collect the ball with ease and beat the stranded goalkeeper.

Oxford might yet have scored again but were forced to replay at Goodison, where a much-improved Everton won 4–1. From then on Everton seemed to believe that luck was on their side. They reached the final of the Milk Cup, and shared two splendid games with Liverpool; they won the FA Cup; they pulled themselves up to seventh in the League. Next season was to be better still. The Blues had turned the corner.

There is no doubt that the match at Oxford was the turning point. Had that goal not happened, Everton might well have remained near the foot of the table, and been out of the Milk Cup, with a manager under fire. They might never have come back.

There were to be many occasions in the seasons following this escape when Everton fought back from apparent defeat with a late goal or two. But on this occasion the late goal was a gift from the opposition. Kevin Brock was later voted Oxford's 'Player of the Year'. For what he did for Everton, he might well have been voted 'Player of the Decade' at Goodison.

Teams: *Everton:* Southall; Stevens, Harper, Ratcliffe, Mountfield, Reid, Irvine, Heath, Sharp, Johnson (Richardson), Sheedy.
Oxford United: Hardwick; Hinshelwood, McDonald, Train, Briggs, Shotton, Lawrence, Biggins, Vinter, Hebberd (Whatmore), Brock.

Opposite *Adrian Heath scores the equaliser against Oxford United, which launched Everton into the most successful period of their history.*

Milk Cup final, 1984

Everton 0   Liverpool 0

The first all-Merseyside final at Wembley was eagerly awaited, and did not disappoint, except, perhaps, in the denial of a penalty and the lack of goals. The rehabilitation of Everton since mid-season was such that for the first time in years they could play Liverpool in an important match with something approaching an even chance. They were already in the FA Cup final, and the song of the fans, to the tune of Che sara sara, was 'Tell me ma, me ma, to put the champagne on ice, we're going to Wembley twice....'

In pouring rain, Liverpool set out to play in their usual confident, patient style, with which they'd won so many games by absorbing and nullifying their opponents' efforts before steam-rollering over them later. But Everton began with such splendid enthusiasm and skill that they could not be contained. After only eight minutes, Heath and Grobbelaar slid in to a pass from Sharp, Heath won the ball, and from a sitting position hooked it towards the empty net. Hansen came rushing in and scrambled it free, using what 90 per cent of the spectators and millions of Sunday afternoon live television viewers could see was his hand. The referee and linesman, however, were in the other 10 per cent, and the transgression went unpunished.

Everton were not disheartened, and for an hour continued to make the best chances. The tide began to turn in the 64th minute, when a Rush strike nearly settled the matter – the ball bobbled on a low cross causing him to shoot over from five yards.

Everton's attacks from now on were against the tide, but the last real chance in normal time nevertheless fell to Sharp, who shot wide with two minutes to go. In extra-time Rush nearly won the match again, hitting a tremendous volley from a few yards out to produce the best save of the match from Southall, who turned it away.

The Blues made the final thrust, when Sharp's header and Heath's hooked shot from close in had Grobbelaar beaten, but the ball hit Neal on the line and bounced into the goalkeeper's arms.

A draw was a fair result. Despite the lack of goals it had been an exciting and skilful game. The years of 'Everton jokes' from Liverpool supporters were forgotten as the fans mixed happily after the match and everybody noted the feeling of a Merseyside festival. Liverpool won the replay with a semi-fortuitous goal from Souness, but the match confirmed Everton's arrival in the big time, and there were triumphs just around the corner.

Teams: *Everton:* Southall; Stevens, Bailey, Ratcliffe, Mountfield, Reid, Irvine, Heath, Sharp, Richardson, Sheedy (Harper).
Liverpool: Grobbelaar; Neal, Kennedy, Lawrenson, Whelan, Hansen, Dalglish, Lee, Rush, Johnston (Robinson), Souness.

FA Cup final, 1984

Everton 2   Watford 0

Two of the friendliest sets of supporters in the country had the pleasure of seeing their teams at Wembley in 1984. Everton's rejuvenated blend of flair and experience met Graham Taylor's Watford, a club of no traditions, currently with a youthful side often accused of optimistic hit-and-run tactics but capable on their day of beating the best sides with their speed and mastery of the basics.

On a sunny day both teams settled down to attack, and Everton generally looked the more dangerous. Watford had the misfortune to be without their captain and left-back, Rostron, who was suspended. His replacement, Neil Price, emphasized the youth and inexperience of the Watford back four. Trevor Steven was soon making effective probes down Watford's left flank.

However, Watford were masters of the break, with John Barnes and the raiding of Mo Johnston always likely to produce something from an apparently harmless position, and the Blues had a fright when Barnes' blocked shot rebounded nicely for an onrushing Les Taylor, who shot just wide.

Neville Southall had to slide to save at Johnston's feet, another Barnes rebound was put wide by Price, and Taylor again charged through to miss the target. Everton's attacks, by contrast, were more methodical but less dangerous, until finally they scored after a bit of bagatelle in the penalty area. A cross from Kevin Richardson was weakly headed out by Lee Sinnott, Gary Stevens and John Barnes barged each other for the ball and Stevens managed to force it back into the middle where the defence stood still as Sharp stopped the ball with his left foot and clipped it with his right into the net off the foot of the post. Watford could feel slightly aggrieved at being down at half-time.

Early in the second half Southall needed to be at his best again when Kenny Jackett's centre looked certain to be converted by Barnes, but a great leap by the keeper allowed him to reach the ball.

Then, in the 51st minute, Everton sealed it with a controversial goal. It could be seen as a typical brave Andy Gray header, a bad error by goalkeeper Steve Sherwood, which had looked to be on the cards more than once before, or a downright foul by the centre-forward.

Trevor Steven floated in a centre. Sherwood had it well covered, but the presence of Steve Terry made him catch it awkwardly, and, left to his own devices, he might well have fallen backwards on landing. But Gray was already steaming in from behind. Even as the goalkeeper caught the ball so Gray's head was there, the goalie ended dumped on the floor and the ball was in the net.

Did Gray head it cleanly? Did Sherwood drop the ball as Gray bundled into him illegally? The slow-motion replay suggested that Gray had actually headed the goalkeeper's hands, knocking the ball from them. Anyway, lucky or not, the referee gave a goal and Watford were unlikely to score twice, although they tried hard and might have had a consolatory goal.

It was Everton's first major trophy since the 1970 Championship – but not the last for their new, exciting side.

Teams: *Everton:* Southall; Stevens, Bailey, Ratcliffe, Mountfield, Reid, Steven, Heath, Sharp, Gray, Richardson.
Watford: Sherwood; Bardsley, Price (Atkinson), Terry, Perry, Sinnott, Callaghan, Johnston, Reilly, Jackett, Barnes.

First-Division match, 1984

Everton 5   Manchester United 0

Everton began the 1984–85 season with two defeats, but on 20 October 1984 they won 1–0 at Liverpool, and when they faced Manchester United at Goodison the following Saturday they stood fourth in the League, with the same number of points as United, but behind on goal difference. If they were to challenge for the Championship, as all their fans hoped since the big revival, this match would be a measure of their aspirations, as well as worth 'double points, as they say. Over 40,000 fans, the biggest crowd of the day, turned up to watch.

United fielded their expensive stars. Everton faced them with the players still regarded in the country at large as competent rather than star material. It was the comparatively unsung engine-room of the Blues – Bracewell, Reid and Steven – who took a grip on the match early on, and determined in which direction the traffic would flow. Robson, Moses, Olsen and Strachan could not halt the advance. Everton were determined to win this one, and all the early 50–50 tackles went their way.

Everton might have led after three minutes when Sheedy, back from injury after missing six matches, floated in a free-kick which was headed back across goal and Mountfield fired over the bar. Two minutes later Sheedy himself opened the scoring, heading in powerfully, but almost as he connected with the ball so his head and Kevin Moran's cracked together. Sheedy went off for stitches, and Moran groggily remained. The long-term effects were, however, that Sheedy returned and after 26 minutes Moran retired with blurred vision.

Gary Bailey was kept leaping about his goal, even having to save a miskick from his own centre-half before he was beaten again. Once more it was Sheedy who scored, cutting in after Bracewell and Heath had set him up to shoot across Bailey from 12 yards. Three minutes later Moran departed and Stapleton came on.

Even a full-strength United would not hold Everton on this day, however, and it was only nine more minutes before Everton got their third. Heath was first to Steven's low cross and turned it home confidently. Strachan and Robson were booked as United grew desperate, but Ratcliffe showed that foul play was not the monopoly of one side as he cynically tripped Alan Brazil, who had broken through.

Although the match was virtually won at half-time, Everton were not disposed to ease up in the second half, but after an hour Sheedy finally went off for good, to be replaced by Andy Gray. They continued to dominate, and nine minutes from the end, when Heath's header was cleared off the line by Albiston, Gary Stevens moved up to crash the ball back into goal off a post. Five minutes later Heath was again in the action with a free-kick to the near post, and Sharp, who had led the attack brilliantly throughout, crowned his performance with a neat back-header into the net.

Everton proved in this match that they now had a side which need fear no other club side in the world. Joe Mercer, watching from the stands, said it was the best performance he had seen from an Everton side. Everton moved into second place in the League. Liverpool, the Champions, were three from bottom. The report of the match in *The Observer* began: 'Perhaps the Championship will stay on Merseyside after all'. It did. It remains to be said only that Liverpool finished second.

Teams: *Everton:* Southall; Stevens, van den Hauwe, Ratcliffe, Mountfield, Reid, Steven, Heath, Sharp, Bracewell, Sheedy.
Manchester United: Bailey; McQueen, Albiston, Moses, Moran, Hogg, Robson, Strachan, Hughes, Brazil, Olsen.

Opposite *Kevin Sheedy slots home his second goal in the rout of Manchester United at Goodison – Gary Bailey can only watch over his shoulder as it goes in.*

European Cup Winners' Cup semi-final, 1985

Everton 3   Bayern Munich 1

On their tenth venture into Europe, Everton made untroubled progress to the
semi-final, unless a 1–0 aggregate victory over University College Dublin is
counted as a scare. The semi-final, however, was against one of the most
successful sides in European football: Bayern Munich. Everton performed
excellently in Munich to come home with a 0–0 draw, and all they had to do in
the second leg was to win. Nearly 50,000 packed Goodison to see them do it.

The match began with passion and commitment – perhaps over-
commitment. Sharp was soon fouled by Pflugler, and from the resulting free-
kick Steven had a chance but shot across goal. Steven was prominent in a
number of attacks, Gray bustled about upsetting the defenders by his
aggression as much as by his skill, Sharp flicked his headers this way and that,
and Sheedy forced Pfaff to save bravely to keep the Germans in the match.

Pflugler and Lerby tackled hard at Sharp and Reid, and occasionally more
than a Sharp look went back the other way – Reid appeared to spit. Finally
Pflugler brought down Gray, Gray retaliated with a kick, and both players were
booked. Gray and Eder then clashed in the air, and Eder fell with blood
pouring from his face. He went off and returned with a heavily bandaged
nose. The Germans were to complain afterwards about the robust play of Gray.

Sheedy nearly reached a long clearance from Southall, Pfaff having to rush
out of his area to head clear. Sheedy tested the goalkeeper with a free-kick and
Sharp headed over.

Then, in the 38th minute, as Everton pressed, Matthaus slipped the ball

through to Kogl, who caught the Everton defence square. Southall bravely advanced to block the shot, but the ball rebounded to Hoeness, who coolly placed the ball past the two defenders who had rushed back to cover the line. It was the first goal Southall had conceded in the competition, but it gave Bayern not only the lead, but a vital away goal. They held on till the interval, and now Everton's task was much harder – to score at least two goals in 45 minutes. A draw at full-time would be no better than a defeat.

It was Bayern's Belgian goalkeeper, Pfaff, who allowed the door to open. After three minutes he dropped a long throw-in from Stevens, and Sharp tapped the ball over the line. Perhaps Gray's presence intimidated the keeper.

Gray it was who, with the crowd roaring the players on, put Everton ahead on aggregate with a rasping drive in the 72nd minute. He was leading the line with a verve which impressed even old Everton supporters who could remember Dean and Lawton. Still, of course, a goal for Bayern would be enough to put Everton out, but by now there was only one possible result. To put it entirely beyond speculation, Steven broke through and drove in a third goal with four minutes remaining.

It had been one of the most exciting nights at Goodison Park. Not everybody was overcome by the general euphoria. The Bayern coach said Gray should be playing rugby, not football. A West German FA official yearned for the football of the past, but as 'football theatre', the Everton fans rated it very highly.

Teams: *Everton:* Southall; Stevens, van den Hauwe, Ratcliffe, Mountfield, Reid, Steven, Sharp, Gray, Bracewell, Sheedy.
Bayern Munich: Pfaff; Dremmler, Willmer, Eder, Augenthaler, Lerby, Pflugler, Matthaus, Hoeness, Nachtweih, Kogl.

All came right for Everton in the second half. Andy Gray puts the Blues ahead on aggregate with a fierce drive from close range.

SEIKO

European Cup Winners' Cup final, 1985
Everton 3   Rapid Vienna 1

Everton were firm favourites for the European Cup Winners' Cup final in Rotterdam on 15 May 1985. The Championship was tucked away, the FA Cup final was to follow three days after the European final – they had proved themselves the best side currently in England, and that should be enough. The Rapid Vienna side were at Rotterdam after losing 3–0 at Celtic in the second round. One of their players had been struck by a missile in that match, and amid much controversy UEFA ordered the match to be replayed. Rapid won 1–0 at Old Trafford in a match where two more of their players had suffered at the hands of fans.

It looked as if the forecasters might be right as the match got under way. The Rapid goalkeeper was kept busy from the start, cutting out crosses, turning away shots, diving at the forwards' feet. In addition Bracewell and Stevens shot wide. Rapid attacks, on the other hand, were rare, and it seemed that sooner or later the Everton pressure would pay off.

In the 38th minute a Sheedy free-kick was headed back across the goal by Mountfield and Gray turned the ball home. The linesman's flag was already raised, however, and Mountfield was given offside. From the slow-motion television replay it looked as if the linesman was wrong.

Towards the end of the half Everton began to show signs of anxiety. Stevens, who had already brought down Weinhofer (the player struck by a missile in the match at Celtic) was booked for a late tackle on Brauneder.

Rapid were happy to be level at half-time. Their hope was to hold Everton, and then bring on Antonin Panenka, their 37-year-old schemer who, although not fit enough to play the whole match, might be able to engineer a winning goal late on.

Soon after the interval Kranjcar got away up the wing for Rapid, van den Hauwe tried to block his cross, and the ball struck the bar and went behind for Rapid's first corner. Krankl, the veteran World Cup star, also tried a low cross, and Ratcliffe was happy to kick away for another corner.

After all Everton's first-half pressure, the match now seemed to be getting away, but ironically Rapid now made an error and Everton were ahead. A bad back-pass was picked up by Sharp, who went past the goal-keeper to the goal-line, looked up to see Gray arriving in the centre and pulled the ball back for the centre-forward to hit home.

Rapid soon put on an attacking winger, Groess, and shortly afterwards, Panenka, and began to open up the game. The effect was predictable. The superior Everton side began to exploit the gaps left behind. Konsel saved brilliantly from Steven, but a second goal was inevitable. Steven forced a corner. Sheedy came over from the opposite wing to take it and the ball swung past everybody in front of goal to find Steven unmarked beyond the far post. He thumped it in emphatically.

In the last 10 minutes there was more activity round the Everton goal as the Blues relaxed a little. With seven minutes left Groess and Kranjcar combined to allow Krankl to round Southall and score. If Rapid held momentary hopes of a draw they were extinguished immediately. Sharp sent Sheedy through and he shot brilliantly from 20 yards out to end the scoring.

Krankl, after the match, said he had not seen such a good side as Everton for a long time. Certainly they had won their first European trophy with comparative ease.

Teams: *Everton:* Southall; Stevens, van den Hauwe, Ratcliffe, Mountfield, Reid, Steven, Sharp, Gray, Bracewell, Sheedy.
Rapid Vienna: Konsel; Lainer, Brauneder, Weber, Garger, Kranjcar, Kienast, Hrstick, Pacult (Groess), Krankl, Weinhofer (Panenka).

E F C
E.C.W. CUP FINAL
ROTTERDAM 1985

Photographic Acknowledgements

Cover photograph by Allsport Photographic
Front cover inset by Peter Robinson

All colour photographs by Peter Robinson

Black and white photographs supplied by:
BBC Hulton Picture Library
Colorsport
Football Monthly
Steven Hale
Terry Mealy
Peter Robinson
Syndication International

NILKMAN
METAXA
CROWN